THROUGH
WITHOUT

A Memoir

by Krystyna Bystryk Szczesny

outskirts
press

TABLE OF CONTENTS

A wise proverb cautions against the consequences that may arise from "being in the wrong place at the wrong time." This adage applies perfectly to the events that had an immense effect on the destiny and life of my family.

Our family history is complex. It has been fashioned not in a harmonious, peaceful atmosphere but by brutal, barbaric despots whose ruthless hands held the reins that etched the sequence of historic events that drastically altered our lives and destiny.

It is impossible to understand the life of a Pole without historical knowledge. To unravel this sequence of events, we must go back hundreds of years.

Krystyna Bystrzyk Szczygieł

POLISH HISTORY AND SPIRIT

IN 1772, PRUSSIAN King Frederic II proposed the first partition of Poland to Russian Czarina Catherine the Great and Austrian Emperor Joseph II. Polish King Stanislaw Poniatowski, a weak monarch, was forced to abdicate, and the country was divided among these three aggressive powers. There was a total of three partitions that resulted in Russia annexing 62 percent of the Polish territory, Prussia 20 percent, and Austria 18 percent. Poland ceased to exist as a country and was wiped off the map of Europe.

Even though the country was dismembered and subjugated, nothing could diminish the Polish spirit and desire for independence. Many uprisings and insurrections tried to throw off the yoke of servitude. Unfortunately, they were unsuccessful and resulted in a great loss of patriots' lives. History has repeatedly proven that the aggressor's goal is to exterminate the spirit of the country it occupies.

The Polish spirit could not be destroyed. This beautiful country with its rich history and extraordinary culture, traditions, and citizens possessing attributes admired worldwide suffered greatly because of its geographical location. Poland had two greedy, cruel, unprincipled totalitarian neighbor nations on either side. Its struggle for independence, however, never ceased.

Two individuals especially worthy of our gratitude for their valor and sacrifice are Tadeusz Kosciuszko and Count Kazimierz Pulaski. Tadeusz Kosciuszko participated in the 1794 insurrection to win Poland its freedom. Despite its failure, he became a national hero. He came to America and fought in the U.S. War for Independence from 1776 through 1783. An act of Congress made it possible for Kosciuszko to be appointed Colonel of the Engineers in the Continental Army. He is perhaps most notably remembered for designing the fortifications at West Point, which is now the location of the U.S. Military Academy, where a statue honoring his service was erected. Kosciuszko and Thomas Jefferson, the third president of the United States, became close friends and visited with each other daily. Before Kosciuszko returned to Europe, he drafted a will and made Thomas Jefferson the executor. The will directed Jefferson to dispose of Kosciuszko's American property and to purchase the freedom of and educate the slaves who worked on his plantation. Although Kosciuszko died in Switzerland, it was his wish to be interred in Poland. Kosciuszko was honored by being entombed among the Polish kings in Wawel Castle in Krakow, Poland.

Another "Hero of Two Continents" was Count Kazimierz Pulaski, who planned the 1768 uprising against Russian domination in Poland. When the insurrection failed, he came to America in 1777 and joined George Washington's army. Washington recognized Pulaski's skilled cavalry tactics and commissioned him as a brigadier general. His offensive plans were utilized at the Battle of Brandywine and Warren Tavern. He was given the nickname of Father of American Cavalry. Pulaski was wounded at the Battle of Savannah in 1779 and died of his wounds. Before his death, he wrote to Congress, stating that he risked his life because "unable to bow before the sovereigns of Europe, I came here to hazard all for America's freedom."

These brave heroes sacrificed everything not for personal gain but for altruistic reasons. *"Czesc ich pamieci!"* We salute your memory!

For 123 years, Poland suffered under despotic foreign dominations. Despite tenacious "Russi-fication" and "German-ization" attempts, the Poles vigorously persevered in their endeavor for national sovereignty. During these times, Polish youth were denied education. Parents were punished for teaching their children the Polish language, but the resilient Polish spirit and patriotism could not be abolished or even stifled. It is both remarkable and utterly amazing that a country under despotic, hostile control for five generations did not allow its spirit and patriotism to be extinguished but kept it vibrant and thriving.

Many Poles immigrated to the United States in search of freedom. For the most part, they were uneducated and lacked skills, but were happy to escape the powers that declared them second-class citizens in their own country. The Polish immigrants were hardworking, loyal, law abiding, and contributed significantly to the development to their adopted countries.

Poland became independent after World War I in 1918. It was an extremely difficult struggle, but the country rose from the ashes like the proverbial phoenix. The country had been ravaged and devastated by a long period of oppression. Although its citizens were ragged and starving, their indomitable spirit gave them the will to survive and rebuild their battered country as a free nation.

Four generations of my family were born, lived, and worked in the Krakow area in Austrian-dominated territory, yet they never ceased to feel Polish. Their lives were filled with hard work but were peaceful and harmonious.

In 1885, my mother's parents, Wojciech and Zofia Grzeslo, lived on a farm in the village of Siedlisko, County Nadworna in Poland. They had four children – Jan, Jozef, Maria and Katarzyna. Jan Grzeslo was born in 1870 (estimated). In 1898, Jan married Maria Bazan, who was born May 20, 1876. They owned a farm and worked hard to provide for their seven children – Stanislaw, Karolina, Szczepan, Adela, Aniela, Wojciech Bronislaw (who preferred to be called Bronek) and Jozef (Jozek).

They were respected and well-liked for their noble qualities, like integrity, humanitarianism, industry and generosity. Their priority was always ensuring the well-being of each member of the family. It was generally known that harming one meant dealing with them all. Anyone connected to them is lucky because they were priceless individuals.

WORLD WAR I

WHEN WORLD WAR I broke out, battles were fought close to their village, and the authorities ordered the evacuation of the inhabitants. In 1914, Jan was drafted into the Polish army. Maria Grzeslo packed her young children and their belongings into a horse-drawn wagon and went to live with extended family in the Rzeszow region. The older children – Karolina, Aniela and Adela – attended school. Aniela and Adela received their first Holy Communion in the local church.

While Maria and the children were staying with relatives, a couple became enamored with Maria's sixteen-month-old son, Jozek, a toddler with an engaging smile and sunny disposition. The couple tried to convince Maria that they could give Jozek a wonderful home. They could not fathom the extent of Maria's love for her son and children. The thought of giving up Jozek was inconceivable, so Maria instructed her older children not to take their eyes off their little brother. She wanted to prevent anything from happening to her son. I am certain that this episode, remembered by the older siblings, was never revealed to Jozek. The Grzeslos always faced adversity as a family.

When World War I ended, Jan, Maria and their children returned to their village. Everything was in ruin, with piles of rubble everywhere. The land was devastated by the fierce battles fought there. Mines and trenches scarred the land. Heartbroken, they could not even identify the exact place where their house had once stood. Was it near that apple tree? They couldn't tell. They were faced with a serious dilemma – should they rebuild or relocate? Jan became very involved in the postwar rebuilding of the area. He was the secretary of the village and made many trips to Nadworna, applying for reparation and aid because of the total devastation to their home and land.

In 1918, Polish independence was formally confirmed by the Treaty of Versailles. The Soviets resisted the idea of an independent

Poland, and in 1920, the huge Bolshevik Red Army attacked from both the east and the west. After only six years of independence, the young republic was forced to continue its struggle to remain free. Two military leaders, Marshal Jozef Pilsudski and Jozef Haller, called the Polish citizens to action, stating, "We can't give up our freedom." This call to action mobilized the Polish army and ignited the fight to continue the existence of the Polish republic. The Red Army was defeated, and the independent Polish republic rose again in 1920. November 11 became a national holiday, known to this day as Poland's Independence Day.

In 1920, when the fighting with the Bolshevik Red Army ended, the Polish government decided to make available, at an attractive price, hundreds of acres of arable land formerly owned by Polish nobility in the southeastern part of Poland. This allowed veterans and their families to own and farm the land and was an attempt to integrate into Poland that part of the country, which was mainly occupied by a minority, the Ukrainians. The population of independent Poland was about 35 million. There were approximately 1 million Ukrainians and Belarusians, each. The main religion, practiced by about 90 percent of the population, was Roman Catholic. The largest minority populations included about 4 million Jews. They and other religious denominations were free to practice their faith.

The Grzeslo family purchased many acres and moved their family to the newly established hamlet Ostoja, county Stanislawow. They farmed the land, and their family expanded to include Tadeusz, Stefania, Ludwik and Piotr. They now had eleven children. Moving to Ostoja was like moving to a new frontier. After the war, it was necessary to remove any mines and artillery shells left behind and to fill any existing trenches to make the land safe for farming. After many months of back-breaking work, with no machines to make the work easier or faster, the scarred land was finally transformed into fields of wheat, rye, potatoes, cabbage, beets and beautiful flowers. Thriving farms, beautiful scenery and a vibrant life followed.

My father's parents, Walenty and Antonina (Panek) Bystryk, also settled in Ostoja after World War I. They had five children – Mieczyslaw, Jozef, Emil, Helena, and Bronislaw. Mieczyslaw was born February 2, 1902. Walenty traveled to the United States on three separate occasions to work in coal mines in the Pennsylvania area. In January 1909, he sailed on the *Prince Friedrich Wilhelm* from Bremen, Germany, to Brooklyn, New York. He saved money and returned to Poland. Although he tried to convince Antonina to immigrate to the United States, she refused to uproot her family. After his third American escapade, his wanderlust dissipated. He worked as a contractor and farmer, providing for his family until his death in 1935.

On September 18, 1926, Walenty and Antonina's son, Mieczyslaw Bystryk, married Adela Grzeslo. Both sets of parents gave them several acres of farmland, as was the custom. They built a house in Ostoja, farmed the land, and acquired livestock. They had two daughters – Henryka (nicknamed Henia) and me, Krystyna (Krysia). We belonged to the local parish, and Henia and I were baptized at St. Jozef's Church.

As mentioned, Ostoja was a hamlet in the southeastern part of Poland that had been offered to veterans after World War I. Ostoja was eight kilometers from the historic city of Halicz, in the county of Stanislawow, and one hundred kilometers from the ancient, beloved city of Lwow.

Thirty-five Polish families had relocated to Ostoja, which was surrounded by Ukrainian villages. For the most part, the two ethnic groups coexisted peacefully until 1938, when the Soviets promised the Ukrainians the farms belonging to the Poles. Then, many violent acts were perpetrated against the Poles by the Ukrainians. In December 1939, our hamlet was threatened by the Nationalist Ukrainians, and the Polish farmers organized groups to patrol their hamlet, especially at night. On one occasion, our family and other families spent three nights hiding in another village to be safe.

Day-to-day life in Ostoja was challenging but fulfilling. Farming with primitive equipment and no machinery was difficult, but our life was peaceful, harmonious and vibrant, with neighbors helping each other when necessary. Holidays were special occasions to be celebrated with our family and neighbors. The biggest celebration was Christmas, when preparations included cleaning the house, baking and decorating the tree. The *Wiligia* on Christmas Eve was the main event of the Christmas season, with the family together, breaking Christmas wafers and wishing each other a better future. There was always an extra place setting at the table in case someone unexpectedly dropped in. The holidays were closely connected to our Christian faith. One festive Christmas tradition was caroling. Young people dressed up as various characters such as angels and animals. They walked from house to house singing Christmas carols. They were given baked sweets as a reward. Walking on crunching snow or riding in sleighs to midnight Mass, singing hymns and Christmas carols lifted their spirits and deepened their faith.

Celebrating Easter was likewise especially important, beginning with the Holy Week, when purposeful preparations such as cleaning and baking began early. Adults would help children color eggs, called *pisanki*. To this day, intricately decorated *pisanki* remain an important Polish tradition, along with the blessing of baskets containing traditional foods such as *babka* and sausage the day before Easter.

Another holiday joyfully observed was *Dozynki,* a harvest festival around the autumnal equinox. Farmers would often work together reaping and preparing for winter. Dozynki allowed them to rest, share their harvest and enjoy the fruit of their labor. One more important day of the year was November 2, All Souls' Day. Prayer and song-filled processions were organized to visit relatives' graves. Flowers, votive lights or tokens were left at the cemetery in remembrance of the faithful departed. It was a solemn yet inspiring day.

A notable holiday that was not religious was the day of May 3. It commemorated the ratification of the Polish Constitution of 1791. The Constitution established a truly democratic elected government in Poland that was the first of its kind in Europe and the second in the world after the United States'. This holiday and Poland's Independence Day, November 11, were celebrated with military parades. My family enjoyed their nation's freedom from 1918 to 1938.

GALICIA – Mid 19th Century

We lived in Ostoja outside Halicz, Poland.

Holiday in Ostoja - family and neighbors. Picture taken May 15, 1925.

Mama and Tata are seated. Stenia is standing behind and Henia, five years old, is in front. 1932

Henia, on the right, with a friend. Babcia is lovingly watching in the background.

Franek and Aniela with 2 yr old Ania on a Sunday afternoon. 13 June 1929.

Henia & I. I am 15 months old. June 12, 1938.

WORLD WAR II

THE PEACEFUL EXISTENCE in Ostoja was shattered on September 1, 1939, when Hitler invaded Poland and began bombing and destroying everything of importance. On that day, the German blitzkrieg struck Poland without declaration of war. German planes bombed bridges, railroad tracks and Polish cities to prevent the mobilization and deployment of Polish air and ground forces. A simultaneous attack by several German divisions rolled across the Polish plains from the west, north, and south, creating havoc. There was a tremendous loss of life and great destruction of infrastructure.

Polish air and ground forces desperately tried to hold back the enemy, hoping that Poland's allies, France and England, would come to their aid and stem the Nazi encroachment. France and England declared war on Germany but did not offer any assistance. Poland was alone again, abandoned to fight this unequal, desperate battle for its existence.

On September 17, 1939, the Soviet Red Army invaded from the east. The Soviet invasion was the result of an agreement signed in Moscow by German Foreign Minister Ribbentrop and Soviet Foreign Minister Molotov. The agreement divided Poland between Germany and the Soviet Union. This was a treacherous act since Poland and the Soviet Union had just renewed a nonaggression pact, signed in 1939, only a few months before. Stalin claimed that since Germany had invaded Poland, it was no longer independent, and therefore he was not bound by the pact. Poor Poland – attacked, bombed, betrayed, and bleeding. Poland had been independent for only twenty years, and now again these disastrous events were unleashed on its peace-loving, hardworking, law-abiding citizens.

The winter of 1940 was exceptionally severe. At 5:00 a.m. on February 10, 1940, with temperatures below freezing, there was a loud pounding on the door of the farmhouse where Mieczyslaw Bystryk (age thirty-eight) lived with his wife, Adela (Grzeslo) Bystryk (thirty-two), and daughters Henia (twelve) and me (almost three years old). My father (Tata) heard a loud command: "Open the door!" Three men with rifles stood at the doorstep. One was an older man in a Russian uniform and the others were a father and son, Ukrainians from the neighboring village. The Russian soldier told Tata that he was taking a census. He had a list of names of the inhabitants and instructed my father to sign the list if the information it contained was correct. Tata signed as he was instructed. Then another command came: "You have two hours to get ready. You are all leaving. A sleigh is waiting outside. You have no time to waste!" My panic-stricken parents hurriedly grabbed items such as bedding, down comforters and clothing, putting them on a blanket that they spread on the floor. We had no suitcases because we were not planning to travel. Tears streamed down our cheeks; painful sobs of despair and anguish shook our bodies. Despite the traumatic situation, Mama was able to remain rational and make judicious decisions. She packed a small satchel with important documents, including a blueprint for an addition to the family home, church documents, Henia's report cards, pictures (some included in this book) and items significant to the family. What a cruel punishment. Our only transgression was that the Soviets wanted our land. This was ethnic cleansing. We were nonpolitical, hardworking landowners faced with a horrible dilemma – what to take and what to leave behind – and only two hours to accomplish this task.

I was very frightened by the feverish activity and started to cry. The Russian soldier said, "Keep the child quiet. Get ready. No time to waste! You are leaving for Siberia!" I kept crying and saying, "I don't want to go to Siberia."

It was Mama's custom to bake bread, rolls or cakes every Saturday in preparation for our festive Sunday meal, so she always had a sack of flour and other ingredients handy. Friends and relatives often visited us after Mass on Sunday because it was a day of rest and a good opportunity to socialize and discuss the latest happenings in and around the village. This practice of hers proved to be fortuitous when we were forced out of our home, not knowing what lay ahead. Mama had the foresight to grab the sack of flour and other portable items when we were sent on our journey into the unknown.

While we were waiting at the train station before being ordered into a boxcar, my Uncle (*Wujek*) Stanislaw found us and asked the NKVD officer why he was not going with the rest of his family – mother, brothers and sisters. He was told, "We can't take you. Your name is not on our list." NKVD is the abbreviation for the People's Commissariat for Internal Affairs and was a law enforcement agency closely affiliated with the Soviet Secret Police.

Only a few months later, Stanislaw was stoned to death by Ukrainians from the neighboring village as he was on his way to get the midwife to help with the birth of his third child. His son was born the day after he was murdered. His mother gave him his father's name, Stanislaw. Soviet propaganda had incited violence and hate among the two ethnic groups. This is but one example of the injustice that we experienced at the hand of our Ukrainian neighbors.

Freight trains intentionally waited for the deportees at the Jezopol train station sixty kilometers away from Ostoja so that there would be as few witnesses as possible to this cruel act. It took a day and a half for the deportees to be loaded into the boxcars. We were watched constantly by armed soldiers. Luckily my family was loaded into one boxcar together – Babcia, Wujek Szczepan his wife Marcela and their son Ignac, Bronek, Jozek, Ludwik, Stenia, my mother, father, sister and myself. Once we were loaded inside the doors were locked from the outside and Soviet soldiers armed with rifles stood outside the door until the train left the station. We were not given any food, only water. The flour my mother had brought with her became one of our only sources of food. Mama would mix the flour and water into a paste. Then, when there was coal available, she would press it against the side of the warm stove, making a simple pancake for us to eat. Mama generously shared these meager rations with family members and others in the boxcar.

We left Jezopol and traveled toward the Russian border. The train stopped at the Russian-Polish border where we were forced to move to Russian boxcars because the Polish railcars could not use Russian tracks due to the different gauge. Each boxcar had a second level of plywood platforms added to accommodate more people. Each boxcar was packed with approximately thirty-five to forty people. There was only one coal stove in the middle of the boxcar. The one small window was boarded up and a hole was cut into the floor to be used as a toilet. It took half a day to transfer the deportees, who were again supervised by Soviet guards with rifles.

That evening, as the Russian train was leaving with the deportees, all the locomotives at the Polish station gave a long wailing whistle. The Polish engineers in those locomotives must have realized where the trains were taking us and this was their salute, a sad goodbye. All the adults in the boxcar shook with sobs, believing that no one would ever see us again, which proved to be true for most people in the boxcar. Some, with God's help, survived to tell this unbelievable and cruel story. In total, 220,000 people, including 38,000 children, were deported during the week of February 10, 1940.

The many stations that we passed on our way included: Lwow, Brody, Dubno, Zdolbunow, Rivne, Sarny, Baranowic, Stoubcy, Minsk, Tula, Penza, Samara, Ufa, Chelyabinsk, and the last, Bredy. A young nun from our hamlet was able to peek through the cracks as we passed the stations and recorded the names. As we traveled deeper into Russia, we saw that the landscape was drastically different from the well-maintained farms in Poland. The villages looked like a disaster had struck them and destroyed the fields and trees. The Soviet state was desolate and depressing. The villagers we occasionally saw were gloomy, ragged, dejected human beings.

The deportation of families from designated villages took place on the same day at the same time. The deportation was carried out by soldiers with rifles and members of the NKVD. This careful planning and coordination indicated the involvement of higher echelons of the Soviet government. The NKVD was specifically known for its political oppression during the Stalin Era. Months later, we learned that these deportations had been planned by the Soviets in December 1939. At that time, the lists with names and addresses were compiled and our deportation was scheduled to take place on February 10, 1940. There were two more deportations. In the end, 1.2 million people were deported. Years later, when the Polish government in exile complained of this unjust act perpetrated on the nonpolitical people, the Russian government used the signatures on the fake "census list" as proof that these farmers had volunteered to leave their farms and livestock in the middle of the night to go to Siberian hell, a creative but lunatic explanation.

The trains traveled mostly at night, and when we did travel during the day, we seldom went through large cities, to minimize witnesses. The Soviets did not want the Russian population to know the magnitude of these forced deportations.

Occasionally, the trains would pull into a station. The door would be unlocked, and the guards would select eight women. Each woman was allowed to fill a bucket with tap water. The men were not allowed to help. The guards were certain that these mothers would not try to escape because that would mean leaving their families behind. At one station, before the train left Polish territory, my Aunt (Ciocia) Stenia, only eighteen years old, and Wujek Jozef, twenty-three years old, hid in the brush and did not return to the train. They planned to return home. At the next station, a guard noticed that Ciocia Stenia was missing and severely questioned my grandmother (Babcia). The guard threatened punishment, but Babcia continued to deny any knowledge of Ciocia Stenia's whereabouts and the guard gave up. We prayed for Ciocia Stenia's and Wujek Jozek's safety.

In the boxcar, we were cold, hungry and desolate. The water in the buckets did not last until the next stop because it would splash out as the train sped toward our destination. We realized from the direction in which the train was heading that we were on our way to a place whose name alone sent shivers down our spine – Siberia. Sometimes, when the adults were overcome with despair, Wujek

Ludwik would ask me to sing. When Wujek Jozek had come home on furlough, back in Ostoja, he had taught me two or three military songs that soldiers sang as they were marching. Most of the time, I would oblige, and perhaps the shadow of a smile would appear on someone's face. Mama would repeatedly tell this story with tears in her eyes.

About two weeks into our exile, I became sick with a cold. Soon, I was burning with a high fever, but the boxcar's water bucket was empty. Greatly worried, Mama managed to reach through a crack in the boxcar wall and break off an icicle. It was black from the dirt and impurities on the roof, but she was more concerned with my temperature. In an effort to relieve my fever and discomfort, she gave it to me to cool me off and satiate my thirst. While I was sick, no one wanted or was willing to sing. Silent despair weighed heavily on everyone's hearts and minds.

The heartless, cruel despot Stalin had placed us in desperate circumstances and reduced us to paupers with all our worldly possessions at our side. Decisions were made regarding our future and destination without consultation. We were pawns in the tyrant's game, and our lives were at stake. What the outcome would be, only time would tell.

Due to the brutal conditions, some very young, sick, or old individuals died on the train during this grueling journey. The Russian authorities told the families of the deceased to leave their bodies by the side of the railroad tracks, assuring them that someone would attend to the bodies as the train continued onward. What cruelty, what tragedy for the family of the deceased. It was too much to fathom. To this day, whether people or animals attended to those bodies no one knows. Experiences like that left many with a deep wound that continued to bleed for years. For some, this remained a lifelong pain on their psyche. Fortunately, our family was spared such tragedy.

Later, as we traveled farther into Soviet territory, the Soviet soldiers would open the door once a day and give us soup, bread, water and a bucket of coal for the metal stove in the boxcar. We had eaten

17

all the food we had brought with us. We had had nothing to eat for three days despite carefully rationing the flour Mama had brought with her. We surmised the Russians had no choice but to give us soup and bread or we would all have died before arriving, their source of labor lost. The amount of food was just enough to keep us alive, and the Soviet republic extended for thousands of miles. It was to this huge Asiatic area – the steppes of Kazakhstan, home of the famous Cossacks – that the civilian population of eastern Poland was deported. Deportees were scattered across the Soviet Union as far as the Arctic Sea, the Siberian tundra, coal mines in Kamchatka, gold mines in Kolyma, and the steppes of Kazakhstan. Soviet author Aleksandr Solzhenitsyn wrote about the labor camps in his book, *The Gulag Archipelago*. In many cases, the Polish deportees lived in camps that were the predecessors of the gulags described in Solzhenitsyn's book.

It took five weeks for us to reach our destination deep in the Siberian north – the region Kazakhstan, city Dzhetygara, Kostanay Oblast (state). We traveled thousands of miles, skirting the Caucasus region, crossing many rivers including the Volga and moving through the Ural Mountains. The last station was Bredy, the beginning of the Siberian steppes. This was Kazakhstan. Its inhabitants were Kyrgys, an Islamic Mongolian race. We were released from the boxcars barely alive. It was March 17, 1940.

People with possessions being loaded into boxcars, Feb 10, 1940.

Pass No. 92; The bearer: comrade Bystryk M; worker No. 673 is permitted to access the territory of the Kirov Mine; Grounds for decision by: the Dzhetygara City Council #3 from 8 Sept 39 valid until 1 Jan 41. Signed by the Director and Manager of the Kirov mine. (The mine produced gold, silver and arsenic.)

Friends and family in Dzhetygara. May 24, 1941.

From Halicz to Siberia

SIBERIA

TO POLES, SIBERIA was much more than just a geographical area. It was synonymous with the suffering, deprivation, starvation and death to which Polish citizens had been subjected many times over the centuries, whenever there were political disagreements and revolts. The cruel, greedy, powerful neighbor nations used deportation as a quick method to stifle unrest and eliminate leaders of patriotic uprisings.

We were told that we would travel in open trucks for another seventy-five kilometers, in minus-twenty-degree weather (Fahrenheit) to the town where we would live – Dzhetygara. More than fifty mothers and their children categorically refused that mode of transportation because it was such a brutal Siberian winter. The guards objected, but the women would not relent. There was an advantage in numbers. Finally, the guards agreed to allow the women and children, including one mother with a three-week-old infant born in the boxcar, to spend the night in an empty and unheated building near the train station. However, the men were ordered into the open trucks as this was the only way to travel. The trip to the city was very long and difficult. The snow was very deep. Often, one of the trucks in the convoy would slide into a ditch, and the men would have to push the truck back onto the road and continue their journey with the Siberian winds blowing. Before they left the train station, the authorities allowed each man to purchase, on credit, boots suitable for the Siberian winter. The boots were made of pressed wool (felt) called *valenki*. Leather boots were useless in the extreme cold because they would crack and break apart. Winter jackets and hats were also purchased. Meanwhile, the mothers in their dilapidated building spread their bedding on the ground, cold, hungry and full of despair and tried to sleep. Guards with rifles kept them company. The next day, the mothers demanded to travel to the city to rejoin their husbands.

They were told that their only choice was to travel in the open trucks or stay in the building. Each person was given a piece of bread as their only nourishment for the day. After the second day in the cold warehouse, the women realized that the authorities didn't care what happened to them. No matter what happened to the women and children, their husbands would work in the gold mine. The women and children were expendable. On the third day, about fifty women and children climbed into the open trucks for the seventy-five-kilometer trip to Dzhetygara. Their journey was difficult and slow – with deep snow, biting wind, and frigid temperatures. The mothers and children sat on the floor and covered themselves with whatever they had with them and prayed that they would arrive at their destination alive. Later, they found out that another group of Polish deportees traveling in open trucks had reached their destination frozen to death. That truly was their last journey.

The women and children were taken to another dilapidated building where they were to live. Each family was assigned a few meters of space – roughly four meters for each four people. The accommodations were plywood platforms with no mattresses. Each family was given one metal cabinet. Twelve to fifteen families lived for many months in each broken-down barrack infested with bed bugs and lice. Each barrack also contained one long table with a bench on each side and a big brick stove that barely heated the barrack. It was difficult to find wood since we were on the Siberian steppe. The families took turns cooking their food, which was mostly soup. A radio receiver on the wall broadcast Soviet propaganda several hours each day, letting us know that Stalin cared and worried about us, among other Communist nonsense. It couldn't be turned off.

Now an unexpected problem arose. No one was willing to tell the women where their husbands had been taken, and the city of Dzhetygara had five hundred thousand residents. The ever-present KGB guards carrying rifles didn't know or wouldn't tell the women where their husbands were. In fact, the men had intentionally been taken to another part of the city to keep families separated.

Additionally, group gatherings were not permitted. We soon began to realize the mindset of our new home. We had to think defensively and to anticipate the evil intentions of our captors. Our value was measured by what we could provide or do to promote the success of the USSR. We were not valued as human beings or families.

The women took matters into their own hands and began looking for their husbands, walking around the city and asking everyone they encountered whether they had seen Polish men arriving in the city. The answer was always no. Soviet propaganda had warned the inhabitants to be on guard because these deportees were criminals and rebels and should be shunned. However, the Polish men were also combing their neighborhoods looking for their families. One day, while a mother and her children were out searching for her husband, they by chance found him also looking for them. That woman lived in our barrack. She came back and told us that she knew where the men were. Mama immediately took me by the hand and we went searching for Tata, Mieczyslaw, and found him on the street. Our family was reunited, hugging and crying in relief. Tata sobbed, "I thought I would never see you again," as he held us tightly.

We were fortunate because our extended family had been deported together. Babcia Maria, sixty-four, along with my uncles (Wujkowie) Bronek, twenty-six, Ludwik, eighteen, and Szczepan, thirty-five, with his wife, Marcela, thirty-one, and son, Ignac, almost eight, had all been deported. Because we lived in the same barrack in Dzhetygara, we could help and comfort each other in this difficult situation. It is important to note that even in the barrack's atmosphere of deprivation and fear, there were no animosities or quarrels, only cooperation. We realized that we were in this unfortunate situation together and were determined to survive.

A child had been born in our boxcar on our way to Dzhetygara. The newborn's pregnant mother had been deported alone with her four other children while her husband was at work. After living in the severe conditions of Dzhetygara for a few months, the baby died and the family was in a desperate situation. The women in the barrack managed to find someone to make a tiny coffin. One evening, Mama, three other women, and the baby's family carried the coffin on their shoulders eight kilometers to the cemetery for burial. They prayed as they walked. When they returned, the enraged NKVD stormed into the barrack and yelled, "This is not allowed! If you do this again, you will be sent to where the white bears live, way in the north!" Previously, when one man from our barrack died, his wife arranged to transport him on a sled to the cemetery for burial. As the sled carried his remains, women, Mama and Babcia among them, walked alongside singing hymns. The NKVD had been enraged, threatening, "You will be sent to where the white bears live!" Generally, women were not treated as harshly as men, and this threat was not carried out. A short time later, the mother of the infant also died, leaving behind four orphans. The orphans suffered the most. When their parents died, there was no one to take care of them. The ten- and eleven-year-olds had to fend for themselves, begging or stealing to survive. Since the other deportees could barely keep their own bodies and souls together, there was very little to spare. These were desperate circumstances, and death was the liberator.

The atrocities endured by the Polish deportees in Siberia included hunger, harsh climate, hard labor, repression, disease, loneliness, and death from malnutrition. Hunger affected everyone. It was a political tool. The Soviets believed that hungry people were easier to control. When friends met, the first thing that they asked each other was "Did you eat today?" If you had had something to eat, it meant that you would survive another day. Hunger combined with hard labor, malnutrition, and disease accelerated death.

The survival of the children deported to Siberia was in serious jeopardy. The lack of nourishing food and constant hunger impeded the normal development of their growing bodies. The emaciated young adults succumbed to diseases and were dying at an alarming rate. In our family, three children were deported to Siberia – Henia, age twelve; Ignac, eight; and me, Krysia, three years old. It was because of our family's constant, loving care that we survived, were able to leave that land of misery where martyrdom was a way of life, and lived into our eighties. Now I am the only family member left to tell our tale.

The harsh climate was unbearable. Our clothes proved inadequate for below- zero temperatures. Hard labor, including ten-hour workdays with only one day off every other week, took its toll. Hungry, hardworking people became weaker and succumbed to diseases such as dysentery, pneumonia, urinary tract infections, night blindness, typhoid fever, and frostbite. Those without medical help wished that death would come as a merciful liberator.

No one was free from repression. Constant fear of being arrested for any transgression the NKVD could invent or imagine gripped everyone. One day, an NKVD officer approached Wujek Ludwik, now nineteen, and asked him to spy and report to him what was being said in the barrack. Ludwik, a highly principled, loyal young man would rather have lost his life than betray his countrymen. He had to be diplomatic with his refusal so as not to create suspicion, so he said that he worked long hours and was not around much. Thankfully, the NKVD accepted his explanation without unpleasant consequences. He could have been arrested for insubordination.

My father did not shave for a few days because he was so miserable. The NKVD began to ask questions such as "Are you planning something?" and "Why don't you care how you look?" Mama begged him to shave because any further suspicion from the authorities could be dangerous. One particularly traumatizing incident was on our first Christmas Day in Siberia. We were extremely sad. We had one meager meal that day. What a far cry from our previous festive holiday celebrations. That evening we sat around the table, softly singing Christmas carols to not completely allow our captors to crush our spirit. Then the NKVD, as if carried by a malevolent wind, stormed into the barrack and started a search. Fear gripped our hearts because any baseless accusation could mean months of incarceration. The NKVD found nothing and left empty-handed, but we felt even more dejected.

Individuals who have never been subjected to such undeserved cruelty may wonder, "How did these people endure two years of such harsh circumstances?" The answer is always the same: we were devoted Christians. Our faith had sustained us in the past and therefore gave us hope for the future. Religion gave hope under the most incredible circumstances, and we deportees made a dangerous decision. We would practice our faith even though it was forbidden to do so. We would not let them break our enduring faith and spirit. Every evening the families in the barrack would sit around the long table and pray. We would recite aloud a litany to the Blessed Mother and a litany to the Sacred Heart of Jesus. We were inspired by our faith and realized how important it was for our survival. It kept us from plunging into the depths of depression – psychologically and emotionally. It may be difficult for us today to understand the atrocities masterminded by Stalin against thousands of deportees. But the power of the human spirit and our faith miraculously helped us to survive.

A nun from Ostoja who lived in our barrack received a parcel from Poland containing provisions, including holy pictures and rosaries. One day, two old Russian women came and whispered a request for a holy picture or a rosary. They admitted to walking seven kilometers to ask for these precious items. They also confessed that when they were faced with desperate situations, they would say, "Hospody pomylujsa," which means "God have mercy." The Communist system tried but could not erase their faith.

Our faith was the connection to our other life and gave us hope that God's mercy would make it possible for this cruel bondage to end. At first the NKVD commander would go into a rage, yelling, "This has to stop. It is not allowed! You will be punished!" The next evening as the praying continued, he realized that pretending that he did not see or hear this was better for all concerned. Ignorance was bliss. One evening when Tata was returning home from the mine, he was surprised to see a group of people standing outside in the dark near the window of the barrack. He became alarmed, thinking that calamity had befallen someone in the barrack. What had attracted a group of people to stand there in the cold and dark? As he neared the barrack, he heard praying and singing inside. The frightened, repressed Russians standing outside the window were silently participating in our evening prayers.

The local population, suffering extreme poverty, traumatized under constant strict control, and indoctrinated in the Communist ideology, did not help the exiles. The Russians were afraid of the severe punishment often meted out by the authorities. Also, Soviet propaganda prejudiced the locals against the new arrivals, claiming that we were criminals, terrorists receiving just punishment. Most of the local population was descended from those previously deported to Siberia in 1920, Ukrainians from Harkow. They were indifferent, resigned, and miserable after being in Siberia for twenty years. They lived an impoverished existence and could not help us.

The men worked in the gold mine breaking up boulders that had been dislodged by dynamite and loading them onto wagons. This was back-breaking work. The workday was ten hours long, and they were only given one day off every two weeks. The Kirova mine was located eight kilometers from our barrack home, and the men had to walk through the steppe to the mine. This journey was especially dangerous when snow was falling and temperatures were very low. Eyelids would freeze together when you blinked, and it was easy to lose one's way and wander lost in the steppe. Wujek Ludwik worked in an area of the mine where water dripped on him most of the day. On his way home, his wet clothes would freeze solid. When Ludwik arrived back at the barrack after each long day, the clothes that he took off could stand on their own – frozen. Sometimes when severe storms were predicted, the radio in the barrack would broadcast a warning message, telling the men not to venture outside.

The pay for this back-breaking work was meager, between 180 and 200 rubles. Wages were paid irregularly and often a few weeks or a few months behind. This created further hardship because there was no money to buy bread. Punishment for the smallest infraction was severe. If someone was five minutes late for work, even in terrible weather, 25 percent of their monthly wages was withheld for three months for the first instance. Any subsequent late arrival to work resulted in 50 percent of their monthly wage being subtracted for three months. A full monthly wage was barely enough to buy bread, but the authorities did not care if or how a person could survive on much less.

Wujek Szczepan became very sick and missed work without a doctor's excuse. The supervisor at the mine reported him to the authorities. There was a trial with witnesses. While it was true that he was not at work that day because he was sick, the medical clinic had been closed that day. The fact that he could not even have obtained a doctor's excuse that day was irrelevant. Found guilty of insubordination, Wujek Szczepan was incarcerated for half a year. It did not matter to the authorities whether his family would survive.

Ignac, Wujek Szczepan's son, was a clever and enterprising young man. He always tried to help the family, especially when his father was wrongly incarcerated and his family had no breadwinner. Ignac never missed an opportunity to put food on the table. He performed odd jobs and on one occasion received as payment two potatoes and two carrots from a Russian woman. Once, Ignac "helped" a chicken wander away from its house, put it in a sack and ran home with it. He always had a keen awareness and sense of obligation to help, even when he was only about nine years old.

Mama worked as a cleaning woman in the local Soviet high school. She remarked that the students were very well-behaved and disciplined. The little money that she earned supplemented our income, but it was still difficult to buy even necessities. Stores had a very limited supply of food. We could not even buy bread regularly. People would form a queue long before the bread was delivered to the store or the store opened.

Often there were severe storms, forcing workers to stay for a second shift because it was too dangerous to venture outside. The snow was deep and accumulated quickly, covering any well-trodden path. It was easy to lose your way and quickly succumb to the elements.

Even on regular days during the Siberian winter, you had to squint and protect your eyes against the biting wind and snow because the extreme cold would freeze your eyelids shut.

When possible, my mother and several other women walked ten kilometers each way to a collective farm to pick potatoes. When we had potatoes, carrots, and bread, we felt better. We didn't experience the gnawing discomfort of hunger resulting from the year-round food shortages caused by the Communist system. Stores never had enough for the Soviet citizens' needs. While the soil was largely fertile, crops were often not picked in time, so a good percentage of the harvest rotted in the field or awaiting transport. Potatoes, turnips and carrots could be seen rotting in mounds. A more efficient system could have saved the shortage problem and prevented people from starving.

All food was regulated using a ration card because the supply was always inadequate. The cards allowed everyone an opportunity to receive bread and the occasional potato or carrot. One item on the ration card was a tea enjoyed by the Kirgis, and thus in high demand. The Kirgis complained that without the tea they would suffer terrible headaches. The Polish women did not enjoy this tea but purchased it on their ration cards to trade it for items their family desperately needed.

At times, Mama and three other Polish women, along with others from Dzhetygara, would travel by truck one hundred kilometers to another *kolhoz*, a collective farm, to pick potatoes for several days. The pay was 10 percent of what they picked. They received one meal a day and stayed overnight with a local Kirgis family. A Kirgis family would host ten women in a one-room hut. The workers slept on the floor in a corner opposite the family, tolerated but not warmly received.

On one occasion, Mama and Ciocia Marcela went to a *kolhoz* to pick potatoes. When they learned that the other women planned to stay for several weeks, they decided that they would walk home after a few days. In the early morning, they set out for home with their share of potatoes. They walked almost fifty kilometers. Upon arriving at the barrack at 2:00 a.m., they finally admitted to each other just how petrified they had been walking through the steppe in the pitch-dark. So many dangers could have befallen them – strangers, wolves, losing their way. It was a miracle that they returned safely with their treasure.

Henia was enrolled in fifth grade. I was in prekindergarten. Mama was glad that her children were given lunch in school. One day, because it was a national holiday, the children in my class received four cookies each. How wonderful! What a treat! I ate two cookies and brought two cookies home to share with my family. Every member of the family had a nibble. Half a cookie was left for Tata. When he came home from work, I told him that I had saved him half a cookie as a treat. Tata lovingly patted my head and thanked me but said that I should eat it myself. He would instead have some soup for supper. Mama always recalled this story with tears because she was so deeply moved by this simple act of love and depth shown by her malnourished child. Simply put, we always cared for each other.

One day, while my mother was working in the high school, Babcia came to speak to her. When she walked into the foyer, Babcia saw the huge statue of Stalin displayed there. She grabbed a broom she found in a corner and began to hit the statue with it. Tears streamed down her cheeks as she yelled, "You cruel monster! We suffer so because of you!" Fortunately, the hallways were empty because classes were in session. Suddenly, a woman from our barrack hurried toward Babcia and quickly ushered her out before anyone saw her outburst. The woman said, "You can be jailed for this, and he's not worth it." The constant worry of whether we would eat today had pushed my kind grandmother to the brink of her patience.

On June 22, 1941, the Germans invaded the Soviet Union, changing the dynamic between Germany and Russia from ally to enemy. Stalin now had a new concern – how to defend his homeland. On July 30, 1941, Polish Prime Minister General Wladyslaw Sikorski and the Russian ambassador to England, I. M. Majski, signed an important pact in London, England. Poland and Russia would fight their common enemy, the Germans, and plans on how to do this must be formed. No decision at that time was made concerning the

Polish-Russian border or the Polish territory that had been absorbed by the Soviet Union. We were left with unresolved questions such as "Is the place of our birth part of Poland or now part of the Soviet Union?" One requirement of the Sikorski-Majski Agreement was that the Soviet government would grant amnesty to the Polish citizens on Russian soil. Another important aspect of the agreement was the formation of the Polish army in Soviet territory. The deportees and prisoners of war would become soldiers and, together with the Soviets, fight their common enemy – the Nazis. Fortunately, we learned of this important information, and it gave us hope of leaving this godforsaken country and our life of starvation and oppression.

One day, Wujek Szczepan was returning from the mine when he met a man dressed in rags. The man approached my uncle and asked, "Are you Polish?" When he answered in the affirmative, the man said, "Stalin signed an amnesty agreement with the Polish government. Get ready to leave, and tell other Poles about this. Do not delay in getting the documents to leave." It was hard to imagine the jubilation that this news created in our barrack. Was it possible? Could it really be true? Never in the history of such deportations over the years had amnesty been granted. We weren't sure that the information was true and didn't dare ask anyone, so we discussed it among ourselves in whispers.

A few evenings later, NKVD officers came to our barrack and said, "*Towarysz*," which translates to "comrade." That word, spoken to us by members of the secret police, shocked us. It meant that they considered us their equals now. They said, "You are free people now. While you can leave Russia, we doubt that you can actually accomplish this." Leaving Siberia was no easy task. Documents were needed, authorities had to give permission, and the train station was seventy-five kilometers away. All these impediments had to be worked out without delay.

OUT OF SIBERIA

THE NEXT DAY, the men went to the mine office and informed the officials that they were leaving and needed to acquire the necessary documents. They said that together with the Russians they would fight their common enemy, the Nazis. The German army was inflicting great damage on the Russian troops and countryside. We were grateful to General Sikorski, whose brilliant negotiations with Stalin made amnesty possible. Stalin, who wanted to appear as a benevolent leader, had granted amnesty to innocent deportees. How ironic! All the deportees in the twenty barracks needed transportation to the train station. Wujek Szczepan, always a very resourceful and clever man, negotiated with a supervisor of a garage for the use of four trucks. He gave him his pocket watch to pay for the transportation and sold other items to make the move easier. The journey to the station was slow. The roads were bad and the old trucks kept getting stuck, needing to be pushed back onto the roads. When we arrived at the train station in Bredy, Kazakhstan, we saw bedlam. Crowds of people were at the station. The newly released Polish prisoners looked like skeletons in rags next to the uniformed Russian soldiers. We were told that we should try to get to Buzuluk, Uzbekistan, hundreds of miles away, where the Polish army had set up a recruiting center. But how were we to get there? The Russian territory covered one-seventh of the globe. Again, Uncles Szczepan, Bronek, and Ludwik found a compassionate conductor who, for a price – they gave him porcelain pots and pans – led them to two freight wagons where fifteen families from our barrack were able to find accommodations. Once again we traveled by train, this time as free people with hope in our hearts. With God's help, guidance and protection, we had survived two years of extreme deprivation and repression and were on our way out of Siberian hell. We didn't know how long and difficult this journey would be and that, in fact, we would travel a total of three months. The train was very crowded and usually stopped in deserted, far-flung stations. We never knew how long the train would remain at each stop and if it was safe to venture away from the train to buy or trade for food or water. At one station, my mother noticed a pile of boards by the side of the track. She and another woman dragged them toward their boxcar despite questions from the conductor. The boards were used to make bunk beds to accommodate everyone. When we arrived in Buzuluk, our hearts filled with unspeakable joy. Polish and Soviet flags fluttered in the wind on the building where our men registered. Only those who have had their country humiliated and crushed can fully understand the overwhelming sense of national pride that filled our hearts at the sight of our flag. What an incredible joy. Was it real and not a mirage? There was hope, after all, for a better future and with God's help our situation would improve.

When the Polish army was established and evacuation from the USSR became possible, a Cadet Corps was organized as an army contingent. The Cadet Corps would be given food and train young men for future military service. The cadets would attend school and learn military tactics and ideology. Ignac, with his parents' approval, added a few years to his age and joined the cadets for two weeks of basic training. After two weeks, Ignac's mother, Marcela, went to the Cadet Corps camp to bring Ignac home. She was told that the cadets had been evacuated to Persia just the day before. A devastated Marcela returned home, crying, "He's only ten years old!" It was probably to his advantage, however, to be part of the Cadet Corps attached to the Polish army because it generally received preferential treatment.

After we registered as a military family, we were told to go to Tashkent, Uzbekistan. It was September 17, 1941, and it was warm. We sold our heavy clothes in order to have some money and bought a few apples and some local fruit. We hadn't tasted these delicious fruits for two years. However, we couldn't stay in Buzuluk because there was no work for us. Again, we were at the train station, and it was difficult to find a boxcar to accommodate us, and we had a long way to go. Wujek Szczepan and Ludwik somehow found two boxcars for us, and we sat at the train station for three days not moving. We ate some dry bread that Mama had saved. Trains had been requisitioned by the Soviet army to use in the war, and there weren't many available for nonmilitary use. Train schedules were meaningless, so no one really knew when trains would arrive or depart. Every oncoming train was met by crowds of people. Families were separated and children lost in the melee.

We were fortunate because we managed to stay together on one train. The distance between train stations was hundreds of miles. The train stations had diners that provided an opportunity to buy food, but the lines were lengthy, and no one was certain how long the train would remain at the station. Wujek Ludwik would jump off the train before it came to a complete stop and run to the diner to buy food. This practice worked a few times. At one station, however, he was still waiting to buy food when the locomotive gave a short whistle and the train began to move. We left without him. We were devastated. Would he be able to find us? Only God knew. At another station, Mama noticed several big bags of grain on the platform. One bag had a hole in it, and wheat was spilling out. She grabbed a pillow case and filled it with wheat. Now we would have something to eat. She was happy that no one noticed her with her treasure.

At another station, Tata got off the train to buy food. As he was nearing the station diner, the train whistled and began to leave, but Tata was too far away to catch it and was left at the station. A second member of our family had now been left by the train. Only two days before, Ludwik had missed the train. The family was full of anxiety. What now? It was up to my mother to provide food for the family. At another station, Mama noticed a mound of something white near the tracks. While the train was stopped, she again grabbed a pillow case. She tasted the white substance to see what it was. It was salt. What a find! It was very difficult to buy salt, even when one had money.

After two weeks, we were reunited with Wujek Ludwik and my father. They caught up to us – God's guiding hand and a little bit of luck helped them find each other first and then find us on the train.

Our boxcar had been detached at one station, and we were waiting for it to move for three days, which allowed us to be reunited. While we waited in the stationary boxcar, we were overjoyed to see Wujek Ludwik and Tata hanging from the side of a passing train. We called to them, and they jumped off the train to join us in our boxcar. Generally, train attendants knocked hitchhikers off of the trains, but luckily they had not been knocked off this one. We were all crying and hugging, happy to be reunited. Many other families never found their loved ones once they were separated from them. The fact that we were reunited at that particular time was almost miraculous because we had to get off the train at the next station, Kamashi. It took us seven weeks to travel from Buzuluk to Kamaszi. Next, we would be traveling down the Amu Darya River.

In a new province, Uzbekistan, we hired a cart pulled by an ox to take us to the river port. We boarded an old, rusty open vessel with a turbine engine. At a snail's pace, it would take us on a grueling journey. We spent three weeks sleeping on our belongings on the metal vessel deck, cramped like sardines. There was no food except for that which we had brought with us. All we had was the wheat my mother had wisely grabbed from the bag on the platform for us a few weeks before. Fortunately, Mama had brought a small coffee grinder. She used it to grind the kernels of wheat into coarse flour. She then added water and salt and mixed it into a paste and cooked it. This was the only food for the entire family. When the weather became cloudy, the adults fashioned a makeshift tarp roof to keep us from being drenched when it rained. The turbines stirred the muddy, brown water. This was the water used for drinking and cooking.

Near my family, a young girl also slept on her few belongings. Mama became concerned when she saw the girl lying prone and crying for several days. She learned that the girl was only fourteen years old and that her mother had been left behind when she got off the train to buy food. The girl was alone and had not eaten for three days. Mama shared what little we had with the girl until it ran out. For three days before we disembarked, we had nothing left to eat so we drank river water.

We were now in Turkmenistan. We were taken from the port to a *kolhoz*. Three families were assigned one hut. The hut was made of thin strips of wood covered with mud mixed with straw. It had no windows, a dirt floor, and no other accommodations. We slept on mattresses filled with straw on the floor. Each family was given one small bag of flour, for which we were very grateful. Mama decided to try to buy some milk from a local Turkmen family living nearby to make a milk soup. She went to the first hut, saw that the door was open, and took a step inside. She was startled to see a camel in the hut, yoked to a primitive machine that ground wheat into flour. Thinking that it must be a barn, she turned to leave, when a voice called out to her. A man stepped forward, and she asked if he had any milk for sale. He explained that milk would be available when his wife finished milking the cow. He looked at her kindly and handed her a few carrots and pieces of local fruit that looked like chestnuts. Mama, startled by his generosity, thanked him and burst into tears, overwhelmed. The Russians had taken everything from us and reduced us to paupers, although we were innocent and had not committed any transgression. We were starving and destitute. Mama was struck with the realization that although people were different from us, they could still be very kind, and we should never rush to judgment.

When we finally arrived at the river port, we walked a few kilometers to a settlement where we were to live and work.

Once a day, we were able to get food from the army camp a few kilometers away. When we brought the meal home, it was cold and we had no stove, so the women in our group decided that we needed a hearth. The men asked the owner if they could build one. The Turkman didn't understand what a hearth was but gave his approval. The search for rocks and bricks of various sizes began. When the hearth was finished, the Turkmen owner was so impressed by our ingenuity that he asked us to build one for his own family. My uncles Ludwik and Bronek worked all day completing this task. For their effort, the Turkmen gave each of them a flat cake about ten inches around as payment. Wujek Ludwik brought this cake home to share with the rest of us. Mama asked him, "What did you eat as you were working all day building the hearth?" He replied, "Nothing." Wujek Ludwik said he had brought the cake home to share with us because Henia and I were also hungry. Each member of our family was totally devoted to caring for each other's well-being.

I was not feeling well and could not use the outhouse, so Mama let me use a chamber pot inside the mud hut. The local woman saw this and went into a rage. She wanted to throw us out of her house because this was considered very disrespectful. We were surprised by the woman's reaction because we had seen a camel brought into a hut to power the primitive device used to grind wheat into flour. Only the intervention of a Russian teacher renting the room next door, who could communicate with the local woman, saved us. The teacher explained that the woman was angry because one could only go to the bathroom in the outhouse. After the woman calmed down, she allowed us to stay the night. The next day we moved to a hut nearby.

The climate in Turkmenistan, part of the Soviet republic, was hot. The women worked picking cotton and the men planting trees for food. The heat at midday and the swarms of flies created great discomfort.

One afternoon, a local woman came into our room, took Mama's hand, and motioned for my mother, Henia, and me to come with her. She took us to her house. We were invited to eat supper with her family. We had a problem with communication because the Turkmens did not speak Russian. In the room, everyone sat on pillows on the floor around a campfire. From a large metal bowl the hostess served a casserole consisting of rice, vegetables, and cubes of lamb. The woman handed Mama an eating utensil – a twenty-inch-long handle with a triangular spoon at the end. She motioned that my mother should take a spoonful of food, eat it, and pass the spoon on to the next person. This one utensil was used by everyone: two older men with beards, a girl, the woman, Henia, my mother, and me. Mama remembered that the casserole was delicious and was grateful to the Muslim woman for her kindness. Despite our divergent beliefs and ideals, she felt compassion for us. What prompted the Muslim woman to invite a Christian family to her house to share a meal? Perhaps our gaunt, malnourished appearance touched her heart.

One morning, we had oatmeal for breakfast. There was enough for our family, so Mama decided to invite the woman as a gesture of gratitude. Each member of our family had their own bowl and spoon to use. This made quite an impression on the young woman. Shortly after, the woman invited Mama to share a bowl of soup. She had regular spoons and bowls for everyone. The local woman proved to be very observant, a quick study, and willing to learn.

One day while we were at work, an official from the Polish government came looking for us. He said that we needed to go back to port for a return trip up the Amu Darya River. We had to get back to Samarkand, Uzbekistan. The men would begin basic training soon. We asked the Turkmen hut owner to take us to the port. He refused because he wanted us to stay. He said that he had learned a great deal from us. There was no way we would stay, so we had to look for help from someone else.

When we were packing to leave, the Russian teacher came in and was extremely sad. He cried and said that he had been so happy to socialize with us because he had nothing in common with the people of Turkmenistan. He wished us well.

We boarded a barge and sailed on the Amu Darya River. The barge was very slow because it had no motor, only turbines. We endured almost three weeks of another extremely difficult voyage. Once a day, we were given a bowl of fish "gumbo" and a piece of bread. The soup was full of fish bones with just a few vegetables floating in it. Eating the soup was hazardous because it contained so many bones. Mama hovered over Henia and me and cautioned us to "eat slowly and carefully." When we reached the port, and disembarked, it was nighttime and we had no place to go. Again, we slept under the stars on our few worldly possessions. Even though the climate was mild, the temperature in the night dipped, and we awoke with frost on our bedding. I was four and a half years old and became sick from sleeping out in the open.

In the morning, someone from the army took us to an Uzbek village where we rented a hut and were told that the adults would work in the *kolhoz*. The adults were paid for their work in bags of barley.

It was December 24, 1941. We only had some dry bread to eat because Wujek Szczepan had traded a jacket for it. We were forlorn. It was Christmas Eve, and we were living the Christmas story – no room at the inn, and we were hungry and alone. The memory of wonderful Christmas celebrations in the past combined with our sorry circumstances made this an extremely depressing Christmas.

I became very ill, so Tata went to the clinic and begged the doctor to come see his sick child. I was diagnosed with double pneumonia, measles, and an ear infection with a high fever. The prognosis was poor, but the doctor offered hope if I was admitted to the hospital. Mama insisted that she would not let me go to the hospital alone. At the hospital, I was given a crib, and my mother sat in a straight-backed chair. The treatment lasted one month and consisted of twice-daily applications of hot cups on my back and chest to relieve congestion. Hospital patients received vegetable soup and bread once a day. Whatever I didn't eat became my mother's meal, since she was given only a slice of bread. Mama saved it, planning to give the dried bread to my sister, who suffered from pellagra, a serious disorder affecting the digestive system, nerves, and skin, resulting in severe diarrhea. Pellagra is caused by a deficiency of nutrients. Although gravely ill, Henia could not be admitted to the hospital because she had no fever. While at the hospital, Mama asked a young female doctor for some cod liver oil because she believed that it would help her undernourished fifteen-year-old daughter, Henia. The doctor said cod liver oil was only available to Communist Party members, but she promised to try and get some for my mother. The young doctor kept her promise and gave Mama half a bottle of cod liver oil.

Meanwhile, the doctor recommended that I be kept upright and not allowed to lie down all day. Mama had to carry me and hold me upright so that I could breathe more easily in the hope that it would clear my congestion.

Sometime in February, the men relocated to Kermine, now known as Navoiy, to begin military training. Uncles Szczepan, Bronek and Ludwik left. My father, because he was older, remained with Babcia and Henia. Whenever possible, Tata and my uncles, before they left for training, came to the hospital and took turns carrying me so that Mama could rest. We were very lucky that while Mama was at the hospital taking care of me for a month, Babcia was home taking care of Henia and running the household while other members of the family worked.

My father had to hire an Uzbek with an ox-pulled cart to transport us home. When Mama and I returned from the hospital, we remained in the Uzbek village. Henia was still very sick with pellagra. She was seriously malnourished, and there was no medicine for this disease. The outlook for Henia was truly dire. Fortunately, God's providence had a different plan for Henia. While it was difficult to live, we didn't want to die. We still had hope that we would survive and make it to a better place.

One day, an Uzbek man came to the hut where we were staying and asked my mother if she would like the hind leg of an ox that had drowned that day as the owner was carting produce to the other side of the river. My mother and the other women were filled with gratitude for his generosity and kindness. Mama planned to make a stew for the family. This was a great treat, since we had not had meat for over a year. The cooking stew filled the mud hut with its delicious fragrance. Henia kept asking, "Is it ready to eat?" With pain in her heart, Mama looked at her malnourished daughter and thought, "She can't survive this disease much longer. Perhaps it wouldn't make things any worse than they already are, and at the least Henia will not be hungry." When the stew was ready, Mama cut the meat into tiny pieces and gave Henia some of it to eat, cautioning, "Chew it well and eat slowly." Henia ate small portions several times a day with no adverse effects. The next day Mama repeated the process, and on the third day Henia happily stated that her digestive problems had subsided and she had a good appetite. The following day, Henia again said that the symptoms she experienced for two months had stopped. She was on her way to recovery. In two weeks, the color of her skin improved, and she was strong enough to walk again. The family was overjoyed. Another child had been snatched from death's door.

Mama received a message from Wujek Ludwik, who was at the military camp. He urged Mama to come there and take home some food and other items that he had accumulated for us. Mama was deeply affected by this news; she knew that this meant that Ludwik had not been eating his full ration but hoarding food for the rest of the family. She was touched by his devotion. This level of love and concern was inordinate and rare in many families, but not when it came to the Grzeslos. Mama decided to travel to Ludwik's camp as he suggested. She also wanted to check on him and her other brothers. Stefa, a cousin, agreed to accompany her.

At sunrise, they walked twenty kilometers to the train station. It was dusk when they finally reached the station and the waiting room was closed. Fortunately, a nearby diner was open where travelers were allowed to stay and wait for the one train that arrived each morning. The diner had one table and three benches. Boiled potable water, *kipiatok*, was available. Mama and Stefa were grateful that they could spend the night in a sheltered place. They slept on the benches, anxious for their safety. In the morning, the cashier opened the waiting room and they purchased tickets. Mama and Stefa traveled two hundred kilometers.

It was dark when they arrived at the temporary military base camp, and they were told that Ludwik had left with his unit for maneuvers at an undisclosed location. They spotted a mess hall and a line of recruits receiving soup for their evening meal. The soldier dispensing the soup motioned for them to come up. They were prepared for anything because they had a cup and a bowl in their bag, and they were overjoyed when they received hot soup and bread. But they had to head home empty-handed. Again, they slept at the train station diner and boarded the train in the morning.

Arriving at their stop, they faced yet another obstacle. The climate in Uzbekistan is generally mild, but that day there was a weather anomaly. A storm blew through, depositing four inches of snow, and they were not prepared. They were wearing regular flat street shoes, and they had twenty kilometers to cover. They walked an entire day wet and cold.

Before they left, the women made a plan with their husbands to help them cross the small stream separating their hut from the train station. The signal was to put a white kerchief on a stick and wave it so that their husbands would recognize them from the other side of the stream and help. Under normal circumstances, the stream was shallow and, therefore, had no bridge. Now, however, with four inches of rapidly melting snow, the small stream became a fast-flowing river with a strong current. Their husbands saw their signal but motioned that it was too dangerous to cross. Exchanging shouts and motions, Mama and Stefa decided that they would find a safe place to stay because it was almost dark. They decided that they would work together to cross the stream in the morning.

The women saw several huts and a windmill in the distance and headed there to see if they could spend the night. Knocking on the door of the windmill, they spoke to the attendant. He told them that the mill closed at 10:00 p.m. and they could not stay. He directed them to a hut to see if anyone knew where they could spend the night.

A man at the hut opened the door a crack, but communication was difficult due to his limited Russian. He led them to another hut, indicating that they could sleep by a wall. He dropped rags on the ground for them to sit on. His family slept on similar rags along the opposite wall. There were no windows except for a hole in the ceiling. The only illumination was a small torch whose flame kept flickering in the drafty room. Stefa was afraid that the flame would go out. She knelt and shielded the flame from the wind to keep it from being extinguished because there were no matches with which to relight it. The other people in the hut eyed them suspiciously because they were not dressed like the local women, possibly thinking that they were Russian officials.

The next morning, Mama and Stefa searched for someone with a camel to help them cross the stream for a fee. They found a man who brought his camel to the river. The camel took one step, felt the cold rushing water, lay down, and refused to move. Mama realized that they needed someone to walk them to the other side of the river. An Uzbek agreed to guide them across for thirty rubles. The two women and one man locked arms and walked across the freezing, raging water to where their husbands waited for them. They rushed home with chattering teeth, quickly changing out of their wet clothes, and climbed into bed to warm up. Babcia gave them a hot drink. The result of their journey was that they both became very sick with symptoms that lingered for many weeks. We were in Uzbekistan from December 24, 1941, to March 25, 1942.

One day, a courier from the army appeared with news. We were to travel to Krasnovodsk, Turkmenistan, a port on the Caspian Sea. From there, we would be evacuated from the Soviet Union. We were glad to hear this because we were worried that as long as we remained in Soviet territory, we would not be safe if Stalin reversed the amnesty decision and did not allow us to leave. This would be disastrous for us. The Polish army began to take form.

We needed to make arrangements to travel to the train station. We asked the Uzbek owner from whom we were renting the hut to take us to the train station. The only mode of transportation was by ox-pulled wagon. He categorically refused because he said that he enjoyed our company, had learned many things from us, and wished that we would continue to live there. When we arrived, we rented an empty room. In a few months, we cobbled together a home, including another hearth, using anything we could find, including scrap boards, brick, and flat stones. The Uzbek admired our ingenuity, but the very idea of living in such a primitive place was not acceptable to us. They were living in conditions that had not improved for a century, so we looked for help elsewhere.

Our men found another Uzbek with oxen that would take us to the train station in Samarkand, Uzbekistan. The journey to the train station took a whole day. The oxen pulled the wagon with our possessions and the older family members and some of us walked alongside the wagon. We now needed to find the train that would take us to Krasnovodsk. The train station was crowded with civilian and army personnel. Some people had already waited for days for the train to arrive, but the trains were sporadic and did not follow any schedule. Fortunately, we found space for our group. After a few days of a bumpy, standing-room-only ride, we arrived in Krasnovodsk. There we waited overnight for the vessel, again sleeping on our belongings. When the transport ship pulled into port, a crowd of people rushed toward it. Before we were allowed to board, we had to face the NKVD, Russian army and intelligence officers, who stood on the dock in uniform, holding lists of names. Before anyone was allowed even close to the vessel, their name had to be checked against the list. Fortunately, our name was on the list because Tata was an enlisted man. The pain of the people who were not allowed on the vessel was evident on their faces. The NKVD roughly said, "Stand aside. You can't enter!" That phrase, "You can't enter," was a death sentence for some deportees. As we had feared, only a fraction of those deported from Poland were allowed to leave because Stalin closed the border shortly thereafter.

Before boarding, as we prepared to leave Russia, we sold most of our possessions and therefore had some Russian rubles. As we stepped on the gangplank, two men in Russian uniforms were standing at the entrance telling us to drop all Russian currency into the basket they were holding or we would be prohibited from boarding and forced to return to Siberia. Tata hesitated, but Mama insisted that he comply. "We can't stay here any longer. Get rid of the money." We could not miss this chance, or we would be forced to stay in a country where "martyrdom was generally experienced" and where we would most likely not survive for very long. Tata reluctantly complied, only to later regret the decision. He dropped the money into the basket.

The Russian government had made available twenty-five old freighters to take us across the Caspian Sea to the port of Pahlevi, now known as Bandar Anzali, near Rasht, in Persia. The trip across the Caspian Sea took two days and was very difficult. There was no food or drinking water, and there were no sanitary facilities on the ship. People made makeshift toilets by blanketing a section of the deck. There was no roof to shield us from the rain. We sat on the open deck of the vessel with all our belongings, drenched. The water was dirty but still had to be used for drinking. Many people again became ill.

In all, about 116,000 people – 75,000 soldiers and 41,000 civilians – were evacuated. The civilians included 18,000 children. There were two separate evacuations from the Soviet Union. The first evacuation took place at the end of March 1942. The second evacuation was on August 12, 1942. We were part of the first evacuation. It should be noted that at that time, Pahlevi was in the Russian occupation zone after the British and Russians had invaded Persia to prevent the Germans from gaining access to Persian oil. The British deposed the Shah and replaced him with his son, Reza Pahlevi.

My father's cousin, whose surname was Golebiowski, died during our crossing of the Caspian Sea to Pahlevi. His remains were tied in a blanket and thrown overboard for a burial at sea. When the freighter docked in Pahlevi, it was discovered that his remains had been pulled by the draft of the ship and were still at the side of the vessel. His body was taken out of the water and buried in consecrated ground in a local Pahlevi cemetery along with more than six hundred other Poles. Divine Providence had a different plan for his eternal resting place.

Typical Uzbek hut.

Ship carrying Polish Refugees across the Caspian Sea to Persia.

Map Persia to Karachi

This plaque is set into a monument in the Polish Cemetery near Tehran.
The inscription reads "In memory of the Polish exiles who entered into
eternal rest with God while trying to return to their homeland 1942 - 1944"

PERSIA

WE SAILED FOR two days. The freight vessel was dangerously over-crowded. As we crossed the Caspian Sea and Pahlevi came into view, it was like a mirage. Green vegetation, tall majestic palms and happy people greeted us. The brilliant sun and gentle sea breeze filled us with hope. It was the first day of our freedom from hell on earth. How different this side of the sea looked – golden sand, blue water, inviting. It was so glaringly different from the Russian side, where the water was polluted with human and animal debris, dirty streets and dilapidated buildings adding to the despair.

As we disembarked, it was a miraculous exodus from Russia. It was Good Friday. Scripture says that Christ rose from the dead, and this was so close to our own experience. Residents still recall the sight of the tortured humans who exited the vessel. We were saved from death in Siberia. Happy Easter! Gloria! Alleluja!

When we arrived at Pahlevi, there were vendors selling fruits, vegetables, cakes, and pastries, and here we were without a penny. Who knew if the soldiers who demanded our rubles were truly act-ing on orders from the Russian government or had been driven by their own greed. Babcia's heart was touched by the look of sadness on her granddaughters' (Henia and my) faces at the sight of all those delicacies that the vendors offered for sale, but we had no money to buy. She decided to remedy our dismal situation. She took her down pillow and sold it to buy fragrant pastries and local fruit for her granddaughters. With a smile on her kind face, Babcia handed Henia and me the treats. Babcia was overjoyed when she saw the expressions of gratitude on our pale faces. Babcia, bless your tender heart, thank you again. She told us that today was Easter. We were homeless, but we were hopeful that God would continue to protect and guide us. Our fate was in His hands. Babcia was a devoted, spiritual and exceptional individual. We spent Easter on the sand in tents in Pahlevi.

A wonderful, emotion-filled Easter Sunday Mass took place on the beach of Pahlevi. A field altar was erected on the beach and prayers and inspirational hymns of thanksgiving were sung enthusiastically. The devotional melodies seemed to ascend as if lifted on the rays of the sun, straight to Heaven's door. Singing reverberated from our hearts. We were filled with gratitude, and our songs were carried over the waves of the Caspian Sea. Christian vocals filled the beach on this appropriate holiday. A Mass of Resurrection was celebrated, and Babcia and Mama were overjoyed. The priests here and now offered the Sacrament of Reconciliation to the faithful throng. Just a few days before the priests had been incarcerated in Russian prisons, and now they celebrated Mass as free men. Some of us contemplated the mystery of life, here on this side of the Caspian Sea. We glorified God with strains of music that echoed all over. On the Soviet side of the Caspian Sea, sadistic, brutal punishment had been meted out even for silent prayer.

The humanitarian relief organizations were overwhelmed by the sheer number of refugees emerging from the Soviet vessels. The people who walked off the vessels in Pahlevi were in deplorable condition – sick, malnourished, exhausted, many covered with ulcers, and looking like walking skeletons. Some people were too weak to walk. This tortured humanity was painful to look at. Accommodations and medical assistance were imperative. The refugees arrived in rags and had to go through cleansing. The deportees had to have their hair shaved off and clothes burned. The humanitarian organizations of the Polish, British and American governments took charge and directed us to a building where we were given towels and a bar of soap. We had to take showers to wash off the dirt and grime of many months. With a bit of our humanity restored after the showers, we went to the next room where we selected clothing donated by many countries under the auspices of the United Nation Relief and Rehabilitation Association, UNRRA, and the Red Cross. The clothes were clean.

They didn't fit well, but we were grateful. Finding shoes that fit was a more serious problem. My shoes were a size too big. Mama found a well-constructed leather pair of shoes that were too tight. She tried a variety of ways to make them comfortable enough to wear. The next stop was the mess hall where we were given food. After the meal, our spirits were even further restored.

Temporary camps were set up for the army and civilians on the beaches of Pahlevi. Here the deportees arriving from the Soviet Union were quarantined. The huge problem of establishing housing, setting up sanitary facilities, and feeding that many people was mind-boggling. The Polish authorities had help from the British and Persian governments. Makeshift shelters and hundreds of tents were hurriedly erected on the beaches – a virtual city of tents rose outside of Pahlevi. Arriving at the gathering camps, we saw the Polish flag fluttering in the breeze and hope sprung in our hearts. Surely the worst had to be behind us.

The Persian government was afraid of the contagious diseases carried by some of the refugees, so all the refugees had to stay in Pahlevi for two to three weeks as a precaution. The army provided food for the civilians, and for the first time in many months, sick people had medical care. Many, however, died in Pahlevi from typhoid fever or dysentery. Every day more graves were needed at the cemetery.

After three weeks of quarantine, the men left for military training. We said sad goodbyes to Tata, Wujek Bronek, Wujek Ludwik, and Wujek Szczepan.

Tata leaving for basic training, October 20, 1942.

Polish refugee tent camp outside Tehran.

THE POLISH ARMY

I FEEL COMPELLED to explain briefly the pivotal importance that the Polish army played in our life and future. The decision to allow the formation of the Polish army in the Soviet Union was a miraculous occurrence. The hostilities between the two allies – Germany and the Soviet Union – now mortal enemies, tipped the balance in the deportees' favor. Stalin became alarmed about his country's independence when Hitler's well-trained and well-equipped army was rapidly advancing into the Soviet countryside, devastating everything in their path. Stalin realized that the solution for more "boots on the ground" lay with the Polish deportees. Thousands of them could be mobilized and help to defeat the Nazis.

Stalin devised a plan to appear benevolent to the world. He declared an "amnesty," freeing the slave laborers (innocent people) and registering them for the army. The deportees were building railroad tracks, cutting down trees for lumber, working in mines and farms, performing difficult work for almost no compensation. They were cold and starving, becoming sick, and dying of serious diseases every day.

To accomplish Stalin's plan, a series of steps had to precede the formation of the Polish army. An agreement was signed in London, England, on July 30, 1941. Polish Prime Minister General Wladyslaw Sikorski and the Russian ambassador to England, I. M. Majski, signed the Polish-Russian Pact. The agreement established diplomatic relations between Poland and the Soviet Union. The collaboration between the Soviet Union and Germany was broken. Now the Polish deportees could register. They volunteered for the army and needed to be organized and begin training. Western and British leaders began working diligently with the Polish government in exile and others to find a safe location where the future soldiers could train for combat to eliminate the common enemy endangering the world's freedom and peace. This dilemma also included the wives and children of the enlisted men. They needed to be evacuated from the Soviet territories. The exodus from the Soviet Union across the Caspian Sea to Pahlevi began.

We, the deportees, were sincerely grateful to the commander of the Polish armed forces, General Wladyslaw Anders, for his far-sighted, brilliant plan regarding the slave laborers in Siberia. General Anders was unjustly imprisoned for two years by Stalin's regime. When he emerged from prison, on crutches, he had a clear vision of how to save many from starvation and disease and how to deal convincingly with Stalin. General Anders demanded that Stalin's government recognize everyone from Poland as Polish citizens and allow them to leave Siberia with the Polish army. This included four thousand Jews, Orthodox, gypsies, Ukrainians, and others, regardless of national origin or religious affiliation. Stalin initially objected. He would be losing too many slave laborers, but General Anders persisted, realizing that when the German-Russian situation was dire was the time of Polish advantage. The Nazi army was dealing savage blows to the poorly equipped Russian army. Another brilliant idea by General Anders was the creation of the Cadet Corps. The very young would register and be evacuated with the army from the land where martyrdom and death was a way of life. The Cadet Corps saved the lives of many orphans as young as eleven years old, who had no one in the army and would have had to remain in Siberia.

Several future leaders of Israel benefitted from Anders's demands to be included in the Polish army. Menachem Begin, the future prime minister of Israel, born and educated as a lawyer in Poland, was sentenced to an eight-year prison term and was freed by General Anders's intervention and left Siberia with the Polish Army. Menachem Begin, along with approximately one thousand Jewish nationals, deserted the army once they reached Palestine. The British were very angry over this and wanted to pursue them.

General Anders decided not to waste time and energy and preferred to spend time training the future soldiers. So much for gratitude. I am sure that Begin never spoke of this.

Many principled Jewish nationals fought with the Polish army at Monte Cassino. Tata had a Jewish friend, and when he was in a threatening situation involving Muslims in Palestine, he showed a medal of the Blessed Mother as proof that he was a Christian and not Jewish. Even in 1941, there was tension between the two religious groups.

The physical condition of the newly formed army out of Siberia was deplorable. They were malnourished, weak after two years in labor camp and prison experiences. When they evacuated to Persia, they had medical help and adequate food to gain strength. Their spirit to fight for freedom for their families and world peace was undeterred. Soon they were ready to undergo intensive training in handling weapons, using armored equipment and warfare maneuvers and were ready and fit for combat. There was a need to train twenty thousand drivers, so they could expertly use mechanized equipment. The task ahead was monumental.

Months before the war, when Germany had become more threatening toward Poland, the Polish government shipped all its gold bullion, approximately seventy-five tons, and many valuable antiques through Romania, Turkey, Syria, and France for safekeeping in England. Two cabinet members, Colonel Ignacy Matuszewski and Major Henryk Floyar Rajchman, oversaw the secret transport. They successfully established the Polish government in exile. The British government used these funds for the refugees, providing food, transport, housing and training of the soldiers. No gold was returned to Poland.

Great Britain was one of the few nations that took exceptional interest in the hopeless situation of the deportees in the Siberian gulags and other camps. We may wonder what the motive, or the driving force, was behind this. The answer was simple – London and all of England were seriously threatened by bombs from German planes and ships. The valiant defense by the Polish navy and airmen spared London and the country from more serious destruction.

An important contribution to the Battle of Britain and, in general, to World War II was not revealed for thirty years. Before the war, Polish secret service cryptographers and mathematicians were able to unravel the secret German codes that were used to send important military orders. In 1932, three young Polish mathematicians, J. Rozycki, M. Rajewski, and J. Zygalski, broke the German "Enigma" code. In 1939, Polish-built copies of the Enigma machine were given to Britain and France. Major G. Bertrand came to Warsaw and took one of the machines to London. The other machine went to Paris. Initially, the British were skeptical but realized the value when they could read the encrypted messages almost as soon as they were sent. The Germans had complete confidence in the Enigma code, and all military directives were sent using what they believed was an unbreakable German code. This was the vital, invaluable single factor that aided in the defeat of Nazi Germany.

Thanks to the success of Polish cryptographers, the British knew what the Germans were planning and could prepare to repel these advances. The Polish cryptographers read them for British marshals as the Battle of Britain was raging. This could be the reason why Churchill often pronounced that "never in the field of human conflict was so much owed to so few." British Chief Marshal Sir Hugh Dowding, the administrator of the Cryptologic Center at Bletchley Park between Oxford and Cambridge, where ten thousand accomplished people worked, revealed before his death the secret that he had kept for thirty years about the Polish cryptologists' invaluable contribution to the defeat of Nazi Germany. Once again, the Poles were not given credit for their contribution. The British congratulated themselves for this accomplishment because it was decoded at their War Center. The British considered it their triumph and glory. The Poles, however, were always guided and believed in the mantra

"for your freedom and ours" ("*za wasza i nasza wolnosc*").

From Pahlevi, the men in our family were first transferred to Iraq – Khanaqin and Qizil – in the Middle East where they were incorporated into the British army under British General Maitland Wilson. They began to train, and their task was to defend Iraqi-Iranian oil fields from the Germans.

In November 1943, after the final training exercises on Mt. Sinai in Palestine, the Polish troops were fully prepared for the battles in which they would soon be engaged. The Second Polish Corps was shipped to Italy in February 1944.

The Second Polish Corps became a part of the British army. General Oliver Lee informed Polish General Anders that the first battle that the Poles would fight would be to capture the German-occupied Monte Cassino in Italy. A Benedictine monastery was on top of Monte Cassino. The Germans were fortified in bunkers and blocking the Allies from reaching Rome by shelling anything that was moving on the main thoroughfare. Other countries had tried to drive the Germans out of their well-equipped bunker, but these advances were unsuccessful. The Americans bombed the monastery. It was now in ruins. There were attempts to capture Monte Cassino by New Zealanders, Indian Gurkhas, and the French in 1944. These valiant attempts were met with failure.

The Poles were given the nearly impossible task of capturing Monte Cassino. The Polish army started practicing special fighting tactics against fortified enemy positions. The terrain was rugged, and the Germans had a clear view of the road and were especially trained for that kind of challenge. They had expert snipers. The first Polish attack was on May 12 at 1:00 a.m. The Germans immediately started their intensive defense, and the fighting went on for hours. The Poles made advances but could not capture the terrain because of the fierce artillery fire and the German advances. The Poles decided to use different tactics on another day.

On May 17 at 7:00 a.m., the Polish battalions went into action with complete disregard for the losses from gunfire and mines. The Poles were advancing. The fighting continued for many hours. On May 18, 1944, at 10:20 a.m., the Polish 12th Lancers Regiment hoisted the red-and-white Polish flag over the ruins of the Monte Cassino monastery. The fighting continued until May 25 when the Polish forces also captured Piedmont Mountain. The road to Rome was opened, and Rome was liberated on June 4, 1944. The Poles sustained heavy casualties. Two thousand eight hundred twenty-two were wounded and 850 killed.

Congratulatory messages were sent to General Anders and the proud Second Polish Corps, and the Lancers earned recognition. General Anders was awarded the Order of the Bath from King George VI of England, the America Legion of Merit from President Roosevelt, and the highest Polish military award, the Cross of Virtuti Military, from the president of Poland, Wladyslaw Radkiewicz.

I am proud to mention that Wujek Szczepan and Wujek Bronek were with the Second Corps and Wujek Ludwik was with the Carpathian Lancers. They fought valiantly. They were among the unsung heroes. Babcia's constant fervent prayers were heard and kept them safe.

Ludwik was trained in Morse code and operated a radio so that communication between military battalions was constant. When it was interrupted, it was his job to crawl, following the cable, to find the break and restore communications. Then he would send a signal to the commanders that the lines were open, thereby becoming a target himself. That function was given to the most trusted, selfless, and brave soldiers. He was one of the chosen. His honor along with his mother's prayers kept him safe.

One incident that Wujek Ludwik shared was how a premonition saved his friend's life. The troops were advancing in tanks toward the area where they would engage the Nazis. They stopped for rest and lunch. Ludwik sat under a tree and ate his sandwich. His friend chose to stay inside the tank. Ludwik, guided by intuition, insisted that his friend leave the tank, explaining that the tank was too visible to Nazi aircraft. His friend resisted. Ludwik again insisted, saying, "Do me a favor – come out." His friend relented and got out of the tank. Almost instantaneously, as though emerging from the horizon, several German planes began to shell the Polish convoy. The tank Ludwik's friend was in was destroyed. Ludwik saved his life.

Wujek Bronek drove a jeep down the steep hills of Monte Cassino, delivering ammunition. They were not allowed to use headlights so that they would not be spotted by Nazi snipers. Bronek was kind, patient, optimistic and hardworking. He seldom spoke of his war experiences. When he did speak of his war experiences, he would relate humorous anecdotes and not dwell on gory war stories. One amazing story was about when he was responsible for transporting three young men to a psychiatric hospital. He was the driver and obligated to keep them safe. He cleverly decided that the best course of action was to make them believe that they were each on guard for the group's safety. He took each man aside, offered him a cigarette, and asked him to keep an eye on the other passengers because they had health problems and must not be left alone. His charges were on guard, eyeing each other suspiciously, and Bronek was able to deliver them safely to the psychiatric hospital.

Wujek Szczepan saw action in Normandy, but he kept his war experiences deep in his heart. Tata worked in military hospitals with wounded and sick soldiers. These were wonderful men – members of the "Greatest Generation."

Ludwik, far right, with fellow soldiers in Italy. 28 April 1945.

Bronek, left, relaxing between assignments in Italy.

Szczepan in uniform.

Mieczyslaw Bystryk in
military uniform in Khanaqin,
Iraq. May 6, 1943.

OUR JOURNEY CONTINUES – FROM PERSIA TO...?

WE, ALONG WITH all the other women and children, were placed in four different more permanent camps. First, we were driven in a convoy of open, heavy army trucks through the countryside where a variety of vegetation looked colorful and interesting. Then the road narrowed and we dove in and out of tunnels. The narrow road zig-zagged, and we passed mountain gorges. The road was dangerous, with precipices on the side and very little room to pass vehicles going in the opposite direction. We were on a road carved out of the Elburz Mountains. The Persian drivers maneuvered the vehicles with deep concentration. One small mishap and the truck could tumble down the steep ravine, and rescue would not be attempted because it was too dangerous. The dust from under the wheels of the convoy of truck rose like a cloud and made breathing difficult. To protect us from the dust, our drivers dropped tarps over the side of the truck. The tarps obstructed our view, and we felt claustrophobic. I felt anxious and at times was petrified. After a few hours, the tarps were rolled up, and we could see the changing landscape. Homes could be seen in the distance. Soon we were driving through the streets of the capitol, Tehran. The camp where we would live was in a suburb. We arrived at our destination at sunset. It was picturesque, with beautiful fig, pomegranate, and apricot trees in bloom. A complex of concrete buildings would house us. We were in Camp #2.

The logistics for providing for thousands of refugees was complicated. All kinds of provisions were needed. We had only the clothes on our backs and a small bundle of belongings. Over the course of the next few weeks, many people became sick with pellagra, typhus and other serious diseases. Here at least, medical help was available but many succumbed to their illnesses. Their new freedom was short-lived. The cemetery outside of Tehran swelled with Polish graves, and additional land for the burial plots was designated.

Since we would live here for some time, certain information about each individual and family had to be recorded. Families were registered. Children were enrolled in classes. Schedules were established. Organized life began for the camp population. Several families lived in each barrack, approximately sixty people. We slept on plywood platforms with mattresses filled with straw. The partitions between families were just blankets hung over ropes. It was extremely crowded and noisy. The food was prepared in a communal kitchen, army-style. The women in the camp helped with the cooking and other chores on a rotating basis. The sanitary facilities were located at the outskirts of the camp, perhaps three hundred feet from the barracks. These were Spartan accommodations, but we were safe.

The third week of our freedom in Persia, now Iran, Mama became critically ill with typhoid and pneumonia. Mama had a very high fever and was unconscious, and we didn't know if she would survive. But here in Persia, her chances of survival were much greater because medical help was available. My mother was only thirty-five years old. A Russian Greek Orthodox priest oversaw her. Mama was grateful for his proficient treatment. He saved hundreds of refugees' lives by prescribing appropriate treatment protocols. The Polish doctors were unfamiliar with many of these diseases. The Russian Greek Orthodox priest asked for no compensation for his services. We surmised he wanted to atone for the cruel conditions and fate the Russian nation had subjected us to. Mama was in the hospital for four weeks. It was touch-and-go at the beginning of her illness. We thank God that she pulled through and lovingly cared for us. Babcia took care of us while my mother was so ill. We were very happy to have our mother home. Two weeks later, Babcia became ill.

Babcia was transferred to the military hospital PCK, Polski Czerwony Krzyz, or Polish Red Cross, in Tehran. She was treated there because three of her sons served in the military. She was well taken care of. Babcia underwent gall bladder surgery. Complications after the surgery caused her hospital stay to stretch into many months. We visited her as often as we could. We had to take a bus and then walk over a mile to the hospital. The street that led to the hospital had many shops, including several toy stores. Beautiful dolls and toys were displayed. I was enchanted by the variety of toys and would pull away from my mother's firm grasp and run to stand mesmerized, not wanting to walk away. I would ask, "Please buy me that doll." Mama explained with sadness each time, "I have no money." She was embarrassed because we were obviously foreign looking. In Persia, women were seen only in male company, and here was a Caucasian woman with an ornery child. Mama had to drag me away, and this scene was repeated every time we visited Babcia. My mother dreaded taking me with her, but she wanted to make certain I was safe, and she knew that the safest place was with her and under her control.

Before each visit to the hospital, Mama would say, "Promise me that you will behave this time." However, the sight of the beautiful dolls made it difficult to keep that promise. Fortune intervened, and a kind woman, whose daughter I played with, purchased a beautiful doll for me. The doll was porcelain with movable arms and legs, had blond hair and bright, blue glass eyes, and brought joy to my deprived self, who hadn't had a toy since leaving Poland.

My relationship with dolls was precarious. I had owned a beautiful Polish doll that my brilliant mother packed when we were deported in the middle of the night, never to return. The doll shared my joys and disappointments. She knew when I was hungry, cold, or sick. She was my companion and brought me great happiness. When we lived in the one of the Uzbek's huts, the doll disappeared. The Uzbek family denied any knowledge of the doll's whereabouts. We suspected that perhaps their religion didn't allow for such human-looking effigies as a child's toy. In Persia, when we lived in the tent city, we slept on sleeping bags, and about twenty people lived in each tent. My family had given me a rag doll with a plastic face with moving eyes and fabric body. On sunny days, we tied back a flap of the tent to let air in. I left the doll on my sleeping bag, and once again someone took her.

After these sad experiences, I couldn't just walk away from the toy store in Tehran. I missed having a doll, a trusted companion. Mama understood. She was always patient and compassionate and tolerated my behavior at the store front each time. One day, another woman gave me a doll. The doll was an extravagance, and she purchased it for me with what little money she herself had. I was her daughter's devoted friend. The woman's husband was an officer whose income was slightly greater than that of my father, who was a private. I was overjoyed to have a new, beautiful doll. I am still thankful to the generous woman for her kindness to a little girl.

While in Persia, we had opportunities to learn about the region and the country. One time we could travel to Isfahan to see the Shah's palace and great mosque. Women in the group discouraged my attendance because they believed I was too young. But Mama, who was a very progressive woman and believed in education, disagreed. She felt that exposing me to new cultures could only be a good practice. She always said, "There will be something we can learn, and she will always remember." And I did. I remember the Shah's palace and seeing all the gifts brought to the Shah by visiting kings for centuries, displayed in a very ornate cabinet. I vividly remember our guide pointing out the gifts presented by Polish kings' ambassadors, who had come to visit the Shah and stay in the palace. I also recall a carving of the All-Seeing deity with four heads. I was awed.

Occasionally, Mama would go to the farmers' market to get some fruit to supplement our poor diet. She would take me along to make sure that I wouldn't get into trouble. The merchants brought their wares on the backs of camels. While they sold items, the camels were lying down and eating. Feed bags hung on their necks for easy access. I decided to jump and sing right in front of one camel. He was chewing and watched me for a while. Mama had warned, "Camels are bad-tempered. Stop annoying him." However, logical thinking for five-year-old me was that I could run away before he could stand up. As I continued jumping near the camel, he showed no reaction. This puzzled me. Big mistake! Then surprise! A spray of feed aimed at my face and chest scared me. I screamed. I was outwitted by the clever camel without any effort. He eliminated the obstacle to his peaceful meal. Mama tried to wipe the slop off me. We had to quickly return home to clean up. I learned the hard way that camels were mean and not to trust their poker faces.

We lived in a total of three different camps around Tehran. As the residents left for their new host countries, the camps would close. Because Babcia was still recovering from gall bladder surgery, we could not leave and were transferred instead to another temporary camp until she received a medical release to travel. We remained in Persia so that she could continue to receive the best medical treatment available. It was in one of these camps that my mother befriended a Muslim woman.

There were two classes of people in Persia, the extremely wealthy and the extremely poor. Mama was an exceptional individual who, throughout her entire life, always felt deep empathy and compassion for the poor, mistreated, and needy. From what little we had, she would still offer whatever assistance she could to anyone in need. A very poor Persian woman with a small child was begging for food. Although she was not allowed to be inside the camp, she would sneak in, and Mama would save food for her and her child each day from our ration. The Persian woman tried to reciprocate the kindness by bringing my mother a flower or a small trinket she had found to show her appreciation.

We had originally been designated to travel to Lebanon. Lebanon, we were told, had better schools for Henia and me and was not as arduous a journey as heading to India or East Africa. Also, Lebanon had a better climate and general living conditions. These were critical, especially for Babcia, who was still recovering. Her convalescence and the restoration of her health was a very important consideration. We were approved for travel to Lebanon but while walking through the corridor of the hospital, Babcia overheard some nurses talking about how Persia was not safe because it was too close to Soviet territory. She thought, if Persia isn't safe, then Lebanon may not be safe from the Soviets either. Having had enough of Soviet rule, Babcia immediately proceeded to the hospital office and registered for the next trip out of Persia (Iran) to a destination as far from the Soviet Union as possible. Babcia refused the transfer to Lebanon and signed herself up for East Africa. Babcia said, "I already experienced Communist 'paradise,' and I don't want to go there again!" This meant we also had to change. My mother had to reassign the family. We would also transfer to East Africa to stay together. She wasn't going to let her mother be without the care of her family.

On July 5, 1943, devastating news for refugees reached us. General Sikorski, the commander in chief of the Polish armed forces and the premier of the Polish government in exile, had been killed in an airplane accident. The airplane had crashed into the Rock of Gibraltar. Sikorski, his daughter, and an aide were on their way to a conference with Western diplomats to discuss the future of the Polish refugees and the Polish armed forces. Sikorski was a statesman respected by Stalin, Churchill, and Roosevelt. He dealt with them as equals. It was his clever negotiating skill that influenced Stalin, freed us from the labor camps, and allowed us to leave the Soviet territory. We lost a great leader who deeply cared for the refugees and Poland's future. Our future was now undecided, and we were still in Iran. We suspected that Sikorski's death was an act of sabotage because he had been traveling with documents detailing promises made by the Western Allies in his briefcase. All aboard were killed except for the British pilot, who was able to bail out and was the lone survivor. The paperwork and signed agreements were all lost in the crash, along with any promises made. The British sealed all details of the accident until far into the future. Even now when the Polish government requests further investigation, it is met with obstacles. How to reconcile ourselves to another injustice? Our faith continued to sustain us and provide hope. The world was in turmoil, and we were without a country. Life continued, however.

Babcia convalescing in the Tehran Hospital. Henia, Babcia & Mama. Kysia in front. October 12, 1942.

Krysia with friend and dolls outside camp in Tehran. December 10, 1942.

Family picture, 1942.

Family picture with Babcia and Ludwik, on furlough,
before being deployed to Italy.

Henia with fellow students in Tehran.

Bronek and his nephew Ignac in Palestine.

TO AFRICA

IT WAS AUGUST 1943, and we were in the last temporary camp near Tehran. Once our paperwork was complete and we adjusted to the change in plans, my mother immediately thought of the Muslim woman because we were officially on our way out of Persia. We packed our belongings, and the trucks arrived. The Muslim woman saw us packed and waiting for the truck. She came running and wailed, "Where will the next meal come from for me and my child!?" Mama was happy to see her one last time because she had already generously gathered some food for the mother and child, as well as some clothes and a few tomans (Persian money). Mama gave her the items, and we all hugged quickly before boarding the truck. My mother would sadly recall, the moment burned into her mind's eye, the woman gripping her child and running after the truck. We were all crying. Our thoughts and prayers were with her.

We would be evacuated to Ahvaz, an interim camp, before heading to East Africa. Ahvaz was located in the desert at the southwestern part of Persia, near Basra and close to the Persian Gulf. The army trucks arrived and took us to the train station, where we settled into the passenger trains. The journey took us through the scorched desert landscape. We traveled for two days. The landscape changed, and then we traveled through the mountains, and the train dove into and out of tunnels. Seeing Hindu military personnel guarding the entrance to each tunnel made us aware that this was a perilous region and time. It was extremely hot. The windows had to be kept open for air. As we entered each tunnel, the compartment filled with smoke, choking us and stinging our eyes. When we disembarked, our faces and clothes were covered with soot. Finally, we arrived in Ahvaz and were once again housed in barracks previously occupied by military personnel.

The authorities in charge of our well-being moved us to locations vacated by troops heading to the front lines whenever possible. That's why we moved from barrack to barrack as they became available. It was a ready place for so many women and children, equipped with mess halls, hospitals, and other necessary facilities.

For ventilation, each barrack had an opening at floor level that measured approximately one foot by one foot, every three feet along the wall. This created great problems for us. We were sleeping on the floor in sleeping bags because there was no furniture. Many nights, a brown arm would shoot into the barrack, grabbing everything within reach and pulling it out through the vent opening. All our possessions fit into two small suitcases, and these thieves were trying to steal the few things that we had left in this world! We had to be very vigilant and protect our few possessions.

Another problem the ventilation openings caused was allowing in sand. Sandstorms were frequent and sudden. In Arabic, this burning, hot desert wind is called *hamsin*. The *hamsin* was like a heavy snowstorm but with sand instead of snow. The *hamsin* would blow handfuls of sand through the vents into the barrack, covering our sleeping bags and clothes. Each time the winds began to blow, we had to block the sand being blown into our area by stuffing anything we could into the openings. After the storms passed, we were busy sweeping and shaking the fine sand from our bedding, possessions, hair, ears and eyes. This process had to be repeated many times during the sandstorm season.

It was impossible to enjoy the outdoors in Ahvaz. The sun was scorching, and the temperatures reached 120-plus degrees Fahrenheit. It was also stifling hot inside the barrack. Between fifty and eighty people lived together in each barrack. For privacy, we again made partitions by hanging blankets.

American and British military bases were located nearby. The Americans were particularly friendly and generous. They gave us candy, gum, chocolate and canned goods, especially to the children. Occasionally, the children were invited to their base to be entertained either by watching children's movies starring Shirley Temple, which were popular and a favorite of many, or by playing games and sports with the men. Some soldiers were very proud that they had Polish ancestors. They enjoyed trying to speak some Polish "as my grandparents had taught me" with us. They happily taught us some of our first English words. If the Americans were passing us on the road in their military jeeps, they always stopped to see if we needed a ride, especially if we were waiting for a bus. We had to use our judgment when accepting a ride because sometimes they were returning from celebrating and were in no condition to drive. In a few instances, accepting a ride meant you had to help push the jeep back onto the road from the ditch.

Thousands of refugees lived in Ahvaz for several months. Subsequently, we learned that the Polish and British governments had decided to relocate the camps' residents to British commonwealth countries including India, Kenya, Tanganyika, and Uganda. A total of forty thousand women and children had to be relocated. Trucks, trains, and ships were needed, but many of these resources were being utilized by the military, so availability was limited. We stayed in the Ahvaz camp for a several weeks. Our final destination would be East Africa, thousands of miles away – a different continent.

One day, the army trucks arrived and took us to the train station, and we traveled for two days. We arrived at the port city of Khorramshahr. The army trucks picked us up at the train station and transported us to our new temporary camp. We lived in tents waiting for a ship to take us to Karachi, then under Indian control and now in Pakistan. We were informed that this was an extremely dangerous part of the world. Three military ships escorted us through the Persian Gulf, the Strait of Hormuz, the Gulf of Oman, and then the Arabian Sea. We needed a convoy because Japanese and German submarines prowled these waters, attempting to torpedo ships. To our horror, we learned that already forty ships had been sunk in the area over the past two years.

After two weeks stay in this camp, a ship, the *Nevassa*, arrived in port, and we learned that we were to be its passengers. The ship was not equipped for civilian travel but used to transport troops. It had hammocks for sleeping. Alternative sleeping arrangements had to be made. Mattresses were placed on the deck and anywhere else there was room – even on tables at night.

My mother had keen insight into any situation. She was a master in quickly assessing matters and determining the strategy that would best benefit our family. She often would go ahead to scout the best location. Directed to go below deck, Mama saw that the dark, crowded conditions there were not optimal. She immediately returned, found a spot near the upper deck and grabbed three mattresses, which were in short supply, to reserve a good location for the family. She told me to sit on top of them to hold the location. If someone tried to take our place or one of our mattresses, I would begin to shout and raise the alarm for a family member to rush over and keep our prized location and possessions safe. As usual, we took care of each other. Other families were forced to go below deck, where it was stifling hot. The rolling seas and heat made many passengers seasick. My mother would often go down and bring friends up to share our mattresses, so they could breathe fresh air and feel better.

Being on the overcrowded ship was an extremely anxious experience. The ship had to remain dark so that our position was not obvious, so lights were not allowed on deck. Our ship had one cannon mounted on the bow and several machine guns on each side. It was an extremely difficult journey both physically and emotionally. Some passengers were seasick and unable to hold down any food. The ocean was angry and rocked the ship. We were urged to follow safety routines and rules. Three times each day a signal sounded, and we had to assemble in designated areas for emergency drills. We were required to carry life preservers when on deck. The portals were covered with black curtains. All of these safety precautions reminded us constantly of the peril we were in and that our lives were under constant threat. There was a priest onboard. We said prayers and sang hymns each day. Again, our deep faith gave us courage and hope. Fortunately, Dr. J. Zamenhoff (Dr. Z.) was onboard, and medical help was available. The good doctor was very busy since many children came down with mumps, an infectious disease. The sick needed to be quarantined, and that was challenging due to our overcrowding. I was a great sailor, completely unaffected by the swaying of the ship. Henia had to lie down because she was seasick. Mama liked to stand at the railing because only the fresh air and sight of the waves made her feel better. Although I was only five years old, I was repeatedly asked to get water for sick friends. Dr. Z dispensed pills for the illnesses, but these generally were ineffective.

One day, grief touched our group and filled our hearts with pain. It was the funeral of Mrs. Grenia, a friend of Mama's from the camps in Tehran. Her body was draped in white linen, and after prayers and blessings by the priest onboard, along with a Requiem Mass, her body was slid into the deep, dark waters of the ocean. We were full of anxiety because Babcia still had not fully recovered and was being cared for by the medical staff. Her decision to get as far away from the reach of Communism as possible had put us on this vessel to East Africa. We prayed that we would all survive the journey.

From time to time, our ship dropped anchor until mines ahead of us were removed. Expert divers spent hours in the water removing the explosive devices, working at a slow and deliberate pace. It was a complex effort, and we appreciated their toil to keep us safe. On one occasion, we did not move for five days.

A personal traumatic event occurred that affected me deeply. Each day, for a short while, I would play with my porcelain doll that I received from my friends' mother in Tehran. She was in a small suitcase with her accessories. The little suitcase was on a table because I had just finished playing, and my mother was about to put it away. An elderly man walked by, stumbled, and knocked the suitcase off the table. I picked up the suitcase to check on my doll. With sadness, I found that it had broken into several pieces. Mama explained gently that the doll could not be fixed. We had to throw the pieces into the ocean. As Mama and I threw each piece off the deck into the foaming waves, we remembered the fun and joy the doll had brought me. Hot tears streamed down my face. It was yet another loss that I, a young child, had to accept. I told myself that maybe one day I would have another beautiful doll with blue eyes. Sadly, I never had another doll. That's life – the good and the ugly.

After three weeks on the water, we began to see seagulls and realized thankfully that we were near the coast of (then) India (and now, Pakistan). At the port of Karachi, we disembarked and waited for a larger ship to take us to East Africa. Before we were taken ashore, we learned of one more distressing event. One ship in our convoy had hit a mine and sunk. Fortunately, the vessel was not far from shore. We were never informed if any of the passengers perished. This was our life full of pain and tragedy.

The stopover in Karachi was beneficial for us physically and emotionally. We could enjoy the beach and relax after the high level of stress that we experienced sailing and the constant fear of encountering mines. In Karachi, we lived in hastily erected shelters with primitive living conditions. Fortunately, this camp was near the beach, and we enjoyed the golden sand and the gentle sea breeze as we strolled along the edge of the lapping water. Each day we collected seashells, starfish, snails, turtles and other marine specimens that the receding tides left behind. After two weeks, the *Orion* arrived in port, and again we gathered our belongings; we boarded the army trucks transporting us to the pier and embarked on the remaining segment of our odyssey.

As you can surmise from the events that I have described thus far, this kind of life was not for the faint-hearted. We were "wanderers" not by choice but by necessity of survival. We had traveled thousands of miles from our quiet hamlet in Poland through Russia, the Siberian taiga, the steppes of Kazakhstan, Asia, and the Middle East, and we were not yet at our final destination. This kind of life needed special endurance. It required emotional, physical, psychological, and spiritual perseverance and strength to overcome disappointments and survive all the divergent experiences and not lapse into despair. Nothing could have prepared us for these unexpected turbulent events, and yet we were handling the vagabond life with amazing grace, patience and…yes, gratitude.

Organizing the resources and transportation of thousands of women and children to their destination involved extensive planning over many months. The pace was slow, and the world was embroiled in war.

AFRICA

THE JOURNEY TO East Africa took three weeks. We were heading back across the Arabian Ocean. Now we were experienced and immediately found another good location on the deck of the *Orion*, while other people were forced to spend weeks below deck. Many of the same situations that took place during our trip to Karachi were repeated on the way to Africa. There were emergency evacuation drills three times a day that each lasted almost an hour. This was exhausting due to the extreme heat and because many people were not physically well. We wore life preservers at all times. Mama would remark, "I don't wish to be saved if my children and mother go down with the ship." Careful planning by the Polish and British governments prevented major problems from occurring, and we had a safe trip. No military escort this time and no mines in the water.

I was now six years old. My curiosity and age sometimes caused problems for Henia, who was entrusted with my safety. As we sailed to East Africa, I constantly wandered all over the ship. One spontaneous and reoccurring main attraction was the dolphins and flying fish that would break out of the water and stay airborne for many feet. One day after the fire drill, passengers on deck called out, "Dolphins! Dolphins!" as they looked over the rail. But the rail was too high for a six-year-old to see over, so I found a twelve-inch hole near the floor of the deck. What a great place from which to see the ocean and the dolphins. I stuck half of my body through the hole and enjoyed a clear view. My sister was already looking for me when she saw familiar shoes on legs sticking out onto the deck. Henia knew it was me and that there was a definite danger of my falling into the ocean. She grabbed my legs and pulled me onto the deck, scolding me, "You always create problems for me! I spend so much time looking for you. Thank God you're safe! Mama will have to talk some sense into you!"

Years later, our roles would be reversed. As my sister's health affected her independence, I became responsible for her care and well-being.

Again, I was a great sailor. The ship was small and did not have stabilizers like modern cruise ships have. Many times, the ocean waves violently rocked the ship from side to side. Passengers suffered from motion sickness and lay helpless and overcome by nausea. It was my role to bring water to those friends of the family who couldn't get out of bed. I would walk on deck holding onto the railing for stability and deliver water, all the while feeling fine myself.

The crew of the ship was from Hawaii. In the evenings, for relaxation and entertainment, they played music in a large room below deck. It was difficult to squeeze through the throng of spectators to see the men play instruments and sing. One evening, I was very fortunate. I was able to work my way inside because one player was looking at me and smiling. Perhaps I was the age of his daughter or relative. He took my hand and helped me to get inside and sit on the step of the stage. I had a wonderful view, and the music was enthralling. Unfortunately for me, Henia saw me and motioned for me to come out. She sent me back to our berth. I enjoyed my special place for only about ten minutes. I was very disappointed and complained, "You always spoil my fun." Henia said, "We will see what Mama decides." Henia was always very conscientious in discharging her responsibility to make sure that I was safe.

Finally, the coast of Africa came into view. The ship anchored in the port of Dar-es-Salaam, Tanganyika, East Africa. Many coconut palm trees grew near the beach and were a delightful sight after weeks of watching only the dark ocean waves and the sky, feeling so small and vulnerable on the ship. We were given a lunch that included bananas, mangoes, oranges, grapefruits and other tropical fruit that we were not familiar with. We enjoyed the variety.

We were taken to a railroad station and boarded passenger trains for an overnight trip to our temporary settlement outside Morogoro, at the foot of a mountain by the same name. Since we traveled at night we did not have a chance to see much of the African countryside.

Arriving at the station in the morning, we were warmly greeted by the native people, smiling broadly and shouting, *"Jambo! Jambo!"* which means "hello" in Swahili.

We arrived in the city of Morogoro. We traveled by open truck to our camp about ten kilometers away. We traveled on dirt roads and were surprised at how red the clay was. The brick-red clay dust rose into the air as our convoy of trucks traveled in single file. The contrast of the red clay and the lush green vegetation made for a beautiful and interesting view. The native drivers tried to keep some distance between the trucks because the dust covered our faces and clothes. As we neared the camp, we reveled in the sight of trees full of blossoming flowers growing on both sides of the road. We were told these were Oleander trees.

At the camp, we saw huts built out of red clay painted white, with roofs made of grass and banana leaves. Each family was assigned a one-room hut. Mama, Henia, and I would occupy one hut. Babcia, who was still traveling with the medical unit, stayed in the building that was designated as the hospital.

The huts had been vacated by British troops. They included metal-framed beds with mosquito nets, one table, three chairs, a kerosene lamp and a pail for water since there was no plumbing. It was primitive and sparse. We were given a schedule for when meals would be served in the mess hall. The names and ages of all residents were recorded. This information was required for the commandant of the camp, a British national.

We slept under fine nets because of mosquitoes, tsetse flies, scorpions and poisonous snakes. Many mornings, we would find these creatures on the nets, but we were protected and safe. Small lizards always crawled through the straw roof. Every evening, we fumigated the hut to repel scorpions, and other creatures. We were advised to vigorously shake all clothing before putting it on, and obeyed this directive. Mama shook her skirt out one morning before dressing and thought it was safe. At midday, she sat down to eat lunch and was stung in the back of her knee by a scorpion that had hidden in the hem of her skirt. The sting was very painful, and the doctor gave her medicine and ointment. One Sunday morning, Henia put on her coat and started walking to church. She adjusted the collar of her coat and was stung by a scorpion hiding under her collar. Henia screamed in pain, dropped the coat and hurried to the hospital for help.

Many camp residents succumbed to malaria. The symptoms included a high fever and sweating, alternating with chills and chattering teeth, which sapped the patient's energy and left them weak and pale. The medications available to us often only temporarily alleviated symptoms. Residents were required to take quinine, atabrine and paludrine tablets to prevent malaria, but sometimes the pills did not produce the desired results. Some people suffered terrible side effects. The pills were yellow, and after a time, in some, caused the whites of their eyes to become tinged yellow. Malaria was a dangerous disease and had to be treated,

The hospital where Babcia was staying was at the edge of the camp. Every evening when we visited, we would sit on the veranda and enjoy the cooler air. In the trees, not far from the hospital we saw monkeys climbing, swinging and frolicking. We wondered about the presence of the monkeys and were told that this was their habitat and that the humans were encroaching on their area. We were also informed that as the camp was being built, the monkeys showed their displeasure by destroying the huts and roofs as they were built. They would rip the leaves off the roofs and damage other completed projects. They also showed their displeasure by digging up the plants in our gardens. Finally, the monkeys were tricked into accepting the change in their habitat. Small stashes of food were left to lead them away from the camp and turn their attention elsewhere.

We were very entertained by their antics. Especially puzzling was one practice. Before they left the trees for the denser jungle, the older monkeys would sit in a circle for about ten to fifteen minutes. The young monkeys continued to play in the trees while it seemed the older monkeys were holding a meeting. After a time, they would line up with the leader in the front, the younger ones in the middle and the older ones at the back and in a single line would saunter off into the jungle.

There was a small stream near the hospital. On one occasion, my friend and I waded into the cool water to look for interesting specimens. Suddenly, I was hit by an object, and I angrily demanded that my friend explain why she was throwing things at me. She replied, "Something hit me in the head too! I thought it was you!" We looked up at the tree and saw monkeys throwing bits of twigs in our direction. We made a quick getaway, not wanting to anger them.

The advantage of living in a camp that was near a city and civilization was that we could enjoy the amenities that the city offered. One Sunday, a group of younger camp residents went to Mass at the church in Morogoro. After Mass, a nun wearing a white habit approached our group and greeted us in halting Polish. We questioned her, interested to know the details of how she arrived in equatorial Africa. We invited her to our camp. She became a frequent visitor and would tell us about the hardships that she experienced when she arrived in Africa at the turn of the century as a twenty-year-old Polish nun from Katowice. Unfortunately, I cannot remember her name. She and another nun had left Germany to be missionaries.

Initially, the nuns were rejected by the natives, who were suspicious of the women. They looked so different from the native people. Most had never seen a white person before. One tribal chief allowed them to pitch a tent and live near the village. The two nuns lived in the small tent, raised goats for milk and chickens, and tried gardening to provide for themselves. Cows could not survive because of the tsetse fly. One day a lion killed and partially ate a goat. The Polish nun used poison that she had brought from home and stuffed the remaining carcass with it. The next day, the lion returned along with other animals and birds to eat more of the carcass. Later, they were found lying dead nearby. The Africans were astounded by this occurrence and thought that she had magical powers. From that day on, they came to her with their problems. The natives were amazed at the woman who had the power to kill the strong, dreaded *simba*, Swahili for lion.

The Polish nun accomplished so much despite such primitive and difficult circumstances. She owned a gum plantation, small hospital, school, chapel and convent where fifty young black nuns worked with her as missionaries. She grew vegetables and fruit to sell at the market in the city. She ministered to the sick. She taught the locals farming techniques to improve yield and harvest. She also taught them how to weave baskets and mats to sell in the market. Such total dedication and devotion to the sick, needy and young was priceless. God rewarded her by answering her fervent prayers. It was her hope that before she died, she would meet and hear her own Polish language spoken. However, when asked if she wanted to return to Poland, she replied, "There is too much work that needs to be done here."

Her prayers were answered when approximately eight hundred Polish refugees arrived. The Polish nun was an honored guest at school recitals, pageants and Christmas festivities. She sat in the first row dressed in her white habit with a great smile on her face and happiness in her heart. In my mind's eye, I can still see the nun in her white habit, riding her bike through our camp. I also always fondly remember the Christmas gifts she brought for the children – rubber bouncing balls made of scraps from her rubber plantation. She was amazing in her energy and enthusiasm, living a life dedicated to serving others. She was extremely happy to see Polish exiles arrive in Morogoro. She said she was grateful and that it was a confirmation that God had heard and answered her prayers.

We enjoyed living in the camp because of its proximity to Morogoro. Shortly after arriving, I had a problem with my ear, and Mama tried to find someone who could help me. I continued to suffer complications with my left ear as a result of the illness I had in Siberia – double pneumonia, measles, and an ear infection. My left ear would not stop draining, and Mama was concerned. The camp doctor referred us to a British otolaryngologist in the city, and we took the bus to visit the doctor. Before the bus could enter the city limits, it had to drive through the gate and be fumigated to ensure that unwelcome hitchhikers were not coming in – like tsetse flies, scorpions, snakes and spiders. Fortunately for me, after several visits and treatments, the ear problem was resolved.

Polish camps and settlements in Africa.

Camp Morogoro at the foot of the mountains in Tanganyika, now Tanzania.

Missionary nun, in white habit, with her orphans in Africa.

.✠ BIBI YETU WA MOROGORO . UTUOMBEE.✠

'Bibi Yetu wa Morogoro Utuombee' in Swahilih means
'Our Blessed Mother of Morogoro'.

CAMP KIDUGALA

WE ARRIVED AT Camp Morogoro in October 1943. In March of 1944, the camp administrators informed us that we would soon be relocated to Camp Kidugala in western Tanganyika just on the boarder of Nyassaland, far removed from any city, six hundred kilometers deep in the bush. This camp was known for being located in the "Kingdom of the Lion" and was high above sea level.

There were twenty-two Polish settlements in British East Africa, varying in size from four hundred to four thousand residents. The total number of Polish inhabitants in all the camps was twenty thousand. This number was composed of eight thousand women, ten thousand school-aged children, and two thousand men of advanced age incapable of military service. Most of these camps were situated far from any city, frequently deep in the bush, some in very attractive, almost postcard-picturesque areas. It was puzzling to us why such remote locations were chosen by the British. The distance from any town and civilization in general created difficulties in the delivery of food, medicine and mail, especially during the rainy season. The distance to the nearest city of Njombe was about 120 kilometers. Trucks carrying provisions would get stuck in the mud since they traveled on dirt roads, a difficult and bumpy ride. The answer to this puzzling question remains with the British colonial government. We were safe but so isolated.

We left Morogoro very early in the morning before the tropical sun became oppressive. We traveled in trucks called lorries with benches placed on either side for passengers. With the tarps rolled up, we could enjoy the landscape. We left behind the sights of civilization – streets, stores, tall buildings – and drove through quickly changing scenery. It was an open grassy plain with sparse trees here and there. We saw many animals, as though we were on safari. A lion family rested close to the road and only glanced at the convoy of trucks. Giraffes, zebras, gazelles and ostriches sped away from the noise of the truck engines. Africa, with its exotic sights and changing landscape, was beautiful. It was irresistibly enticing. An older woman remarked, "I read about all of this in the book by Henryk Sienkiewicz titled *Letters from Africa*." It was a hard, uncomfortable ride. The drivers kept a good distance apart because the wind blew a cloud of dust in our faces. If we let down the tarps, the trucks became stifling hot, since there were no windows to let in fresh air. The road narrowed, zigzagged, and wound as we drove up hills with a precipice on one side. Henia suffered from motion sickness. A passenger in our truck anxiously said, "One wrong turn and we will be at the bottom of the ravine!" We drove for hours, enjoying the exotic beauty and changing landscape of Africa.

When we reached the bottom of the hill, dusk began to veil the African wilderness. We arrived at the German mission of Tosamanga. This was a well-developed mission. We saw gardens, orchards full of fruit and flowers everywhere. We stayed there one night. The missionaries were very welcoming. We were served a delicious meal and slept in a barrack. Very early the next morning after breakfast, we continued our safari. We were fascinated by the beauty of Africa. Many kilometers later, we again started to drive on mountainous, narrow roads. We were approaching our new camp. We saw trees and lush vegetation flourishing because of the frequent rain storms and sunny days. It was the location where lions roamed.

Camp Kidugala was carved out of the jungle. It was in a valley between a hill and a mountain. The climate there was a bit cooler and there were no scorpions or tsetse flies.

The camps were organized in a generic style, and Camp Kidugala housed between eight hundred and one thousand Polish residents. At the center of the camp was a church. Our religion was central to our life, and joyous and sad celebrations were observed there. In the back of the church, fenced off, was the cemetery, tranquil and secluded. The other buildings in the center of camp included school buildings, a recreation hall and a theater where live performances and concerts were given. The most impressive building was the residence of the British army officer who commanded the camp. The general management and administration was under Polish control. The administrative building and general store were also located near the center of the camp, along with several mixed-use buildings. Soccer fields were located on the outskirts of camp where scouting activities and campfires were frequently enjoyed.

Each family was assigned a hut built of bricks baked in the sun. The huts had thatched roofs made of palm leaves and elephant grass. There was no ceiling and only one window, which was just an opening two feet high by three feet wide, with a shutter to close at night, no glass. It was necessary to fashion a screen to keep the flies, insects and mosquitoes from coming indoors. Mama realized that we also needed a ceiling for safety. She used blankets that had been given to us and enlisted the help of an enterprising person to nail the blankets and make a ceiling for our protection. The floor was just pounded-down dirt. We spread straw mats on the floor to make it more livable and to give the appearance of a carpet. There was no electricity. There was no plumbing. We had to bring water in a bucket for drinking and washing. The bathroom facilities and latrines were some distance away. We could take showers at the bathhouse where a generator heated water at certain times during the day. It was a quarter mile from our hut to the bathhouse.

Our beds were metal frames with sisal ropes connecting the frames. The mattresses were filled with straw. Above each bed hung mosquito nets that were rolled up in the daytime and hung loose at night around us as we slept. Many times, in the morning, we would find a lizard, spider, or even a small snake resting on the mosquito net. Very often termites chewed on the floor mats and built mounds somewhere in the hut that we had to knock down in the morning. Each hut had a picnic table and a chair for each person. There were no other pieces of furniture. Our clothes hung on pegs on the wall or were kept in suitcases that acted as our dresser. We were given blankets, sheets and pillows along with some flatware, plates and serving dishes. We also had a kerosene lamp to dispel the darkness at night and by which we completed most of our homework. It was not unusual to see a lizard scampering on the wall or to have one fall onto a book on our laps as we were doing our school assignments. The lizards were harmless to us, and they ate the insects.

Among the one thousand camp residents were individuals with exceptional organizational skills and fertile imaginations. We lived as if we were on an island far removed from civilization and the many amenities that come with it. These remarkable adults and teachers made a great effort to organize activities that would interest and stimulate the young people far removed from the civilized world, and so the camp's social and cultural life flourished. Committees were formed to organize cultural events, sporting activities, lectures, concerts, theatrical performances, and scouting to enrich our lives, in spite of the difficulties our primitive circumstances presented. Other activities included crafts and choir practice. These ventures improved the quality of our life and made it vivacious, vibrant and thriving. The resources were limited, but the knowledge and skills gained were bountiful, beneficial and enhanced self-improvement and self-confidence. The advantage of such a life was that we were a community of dedicated mothers, children, and a few old men too old for service. Isolated but safe, we were far removed from the evils that civilization can expose young people to.

The community celebrated all church and Polish national holidays with Masses, rallies and parades. It was in Kidugala that I received my First Holy Communion. The Bishop arrived for that joyous occasion, and with special dispensation, we also received the Sacrament of Confirmation on that day. Festive celebrations of historical importance were celebrated, like May 3, 1791, when a democratic government in Poland was ratified, the second democracy in the world after the United States. The camp had a priest who celebrated Mass every day and religious holidays were observed. We were deeply religious people. Every family had a father, son, or brother in the military, actively fighting the Nazis in Europe. Masses and prayers were continuously offered for their safe return. Babcia walked half a mile to church every day for Mass. She was very devout and prayed for her three sons who were in military service and her one son-in-law, my father. Babcia prayed and hoped that at the war's end she would welcome and embrace her hero sons upon their return.

The first few weeks of living exposed, unrepressed in the African bush were emotion-filled. When we lived in Morogoro, we did not experience the cacophony of sounds that filled our nights in Kidugala. Because we were surrounded by untamed nature, our camp was like an oasis. At night, the jungle and the savannah resounded with strange, frightening noises – the screeches of the night birds, the crying howls of the hyenas, the beating of drums and at intervals the loud screams of the natives. After the darkness enveloped the countryside, the "African concert" began. All these unfamiliar sounds created anxiety in us. We heard the drums and wondered what message was being conveyed.

Weekends were especially unnerving. The natives who worked in our camp lived in their own villages about a half mile on each sides of our camp. They celebrated *goma*. They drank *pombe*, alcohol made from fermented millet, or *ulanzi*, made from the fermented juice of special, young bamboo shoots. They also smoked the leaves of special plants that had a narcotic effect on the smokers. What they called *goma* was a party, and the whole village participated. They danced, jumped, beat drums and screamed, and the night air resounded with the wild rhythm. It took a long time for the camp residents to accept this as a way of life on the Dark Continent, this spooky, exotic, untamed place.

Camp Kidugala was in Masai territory. Masai are tall and slim-built, with an enviable posture. They usually carry items on their heads so that their hands remain free. Perfect balance is required to not lose their loads. The camp residents had to learn some Swahili to be able to communicate with the Masai.

92

Our meals were once again prepared in a communal kitchen. The kitchen had a primitive wood- or coal-burning stove. The stove was simply a metal plate resting on a pile of bricks on both sides. Food was cooked in big metal pots. The dining area only had a roof supported by posts, benches and tables. There were no walls. Flies and mosquitoes were troublesome as we were trying to eat our meals. The camp inhabitants could eat in the dining area or, as most preferred, take their food back to their huts to eat as a family. Water was heated on the stove and we would bring a pail back to our hut each evening to wash up before retiring at night.

Academics were stressed. Schools were located in separate barracks, and each classroom was furnished with tables, benches and a blackboard. We walked three-quarters of a mile to school because our house was at the outskirts of the compound. Children were registered in age-appropriate grades. Instruction of subject matter was in Polish, with English as a second language. The teaching program was seriously hampered by the shortage of textbooks for students, as well as teachers, reference books, writing materials, pencils and other supplies. School administrators worked with the National Catholic Relief Organization from the United States to request maps, globes, board games and more school supplies. These were appreciated by all, but the students still had to share books. Eventually, a modest library was established with reference materials, teaching tools, visuals, and equipment. The women teachers were totally dedicated, although some teachers lacked proper credentials. Teachers exercised a great deal of influence on the formation of good, ethical, moral, self-disciplined character development. Henia and I attended school. Henia was a student in high school, and I started first grade in Kidugala.

It was possible to find work in the camp. Assistance was needed in the hospital, in the kitchen to prepare meals, and to run education workshops. Willing and able workers were always needed. Finding work outside the camp was discouraged. My mother worked as a seamstress. They used old-fashioned sewing machines and made uniforms for students. Camp residents were encouraged to learn a variety of trades. Instruction in various trades was available, including nursing, dressmaking, and playing music.

Fortunately for the residents of the camps, each camp had its own physician, clinic, and nurses to assist in the care of the sick. The physicians from the transport ship, Dr. Julian Zamenhoff (Dr. Z) and his wife, Dr. Olga Nietupska, were the doctors in Camp Kidugala. The medical care was adequate, but the camps still had serious problems with malaria.

During our time in East Africa, we had to wear cork helmets. The African sun near the Equator was strong, especially in the summer. We were also instructed to rest during the tropical hours. Between 11:00 a.m. and 3:00 p.m., we were encouraged to stay indoors and rest to prevent heat stroke. Several adults were paid to enforce these rules, and if you did not observe tropical hours or wear your helmet, a fine of twenty-five cents was imposed on those who did not comply.

Our drinking water was supplied by the rain. The rain was collected in troughs located around the camp. Occasionally, a snake was found in the water trough, caught along with the rain.

Just like in Persia, Mama found someone who needed help. Most of the indigenous people were not allowed into camp because of their attire. Most wore only loin cloths due to the extreme heat. Some locals worked in the camp regularly. They were required to wear Western-style clothes. One local man named Jozef worked in the camp chopping wood. After a while, he even learned to speak a little Polish. Worrying about our nutrition, Mama would arrange for Jozef to sell us some goat's milk and an egg or two when they were available. She paid him in coins. The locals did not want paper money because they usually buried the coins, saving them to buy a wife.

From time to time, a dentist would arrive with a trailer and stay at the camp for several weeks to provide dental care. One day, in my first-grade class, the dentist checked our teeth. Everyone's teeth were fine except for mine and a classmate's. I was given a note to take to my mother. It had an appointment time on it. Mama and I walked resolutely to the dentist for my first appointment. In his office, there was a chair for the patient and a stand with a drill to be used to prepare the tooth for filling. He used a pedal to make the drill work because there was no electricity. There was no cool water squirting to soothe the tooth, and no anesthetic was used. Mama had to hold me down because it was such a painful experience. One cavity was filled. Unfortunately for me, I had another cavity to be worked on. My mother tried a variety of ways to persuade me to willingly go back to the dentist, including bribery and threats, to no avail. Finally, Mama pulled me by the hand and dragged me on my heels all the way to the dentist's office. I wouldn't wish this experience on anyone, child or adult. It was too painful! I made numerous trips to the dentist's chair as I was growing up. Then I realized the importance of healthy teeth and tried to avoid anything that might result in a return trip.

One of the streets of Kidugala near the center of camp.

The bridge over the river that divided the camp into two parts.

Family picture with Babcia in Kidugala, June 8, 1945.

Henia with fellow classmates, third year of high school.

First Holy Communion group outside the church with visiting clergy, 1946.

Krysia making her First Holy Communion, 1946.

Henia and Krysia holding their cat, 1946.

Henia, Mama & I wearing obligatory pith helmets outside our hut, 1946.

Lions were one of the hazards of life
in Kidugala.

Masai warriors.

MORE KIDUGALA

A MAKESHIFT BRIDGE connected the two sections of Camp Kidugala. Henia and I walked about three-quarters of a mile over the bridge to school, which was near the center of the camp. On my way home, I often found something that fascinated me. Once, several centipedes were on my path. When poked, they curled up into spirals. They were shiny and black with about one hundred red legs. They looked interesting to me. I picked up about five and carried them in my hands to show my mother. I didn't know that she had a phobia about snakes, centipedes and other creatures. When I proudly showed her my find, she became petrified and loudly protested, "Take them out! It's enough that these creatures crawl inside on their own and you bring more home!" They looked so pretty to me, and my mother didn't recognize their beauty.

Another find on the way home was a chameleon. I carried him home, and my mother didn't object when I placed him on a tall plant growing in the small garden patch in front of our hut. He brought my friends and me great joy. We loved watching him change colors, his special talent. He was our science project. We would place him in different locations and watch as he blended with the environment. His barrel-like eyes would rotate to look at something behind him since he couldn't move his head to the side. Mama helped by catching flies. When a fly was placed on the leaf in front of him, his tongue would quickly snatch it. It was surprising that he remained on the plant for three days. Mama appealed to my softer side and said that he probably missed his family and that I should take him back to the spot where I found him. The next day, I took him with me when I walked to school. I felt sad as I said, "Goodbye, friend," and left him on the path.

Twice a week Mama was able to buy milk. She worried because she felt that our diet lacked necessary nourishment. The farm where cows were raised was many kilometers away from the camp. Insects in the area were dangerous to the cows' health and survival. Couriers used large stainless-steel canteens to transport the milk into camp. A courier would carry the canteens on his back a certain distance to a prescribed location. There he would be met by another courier. The milk would be handed off, and the second courier would take his turn carrying it. Three couriers were needed to finally deliver the container to the camp kitchen. One day, Mama told me to pick up the milk. We had a homemade pail – a big empty can that previously held beans, which now had a wire handle attached to simulate a pail. I happily went to get the milk, and a friend came along with me. We waited for an hour, and the courier never arrived. No one knew the reason. On the way home, my friend and I stood on the bridge and noticed many tadpoles darting in and out of the clumps of grass. I decided that it would be interesting to bring several tadpoles home in my pail. Mama was less than enthusiastic to see the pail used as an aquarium. She ordered me to take them back to the river immediately and scolded me for misusing the pail. The expedition for milk did not end well for me. Mama questioned my judgment and ability to discern right from wrong in our primitive circumstances. Oh well, next time I'd leave the tadpoles alone. I'd just observe their antics from the bridge. The reason why the milk did not arrive was explained the next day. The second courier found the third attacked and killed by a wild animal, the overturned canteen lying near his body. There was great danger as well as beauty in untamed Africa.

Vultures were an annoyance of a different kind. They were upon you in a flash. Since all meals were prepared in the communal kitchen, we typically brought food back to our hut and ate there as a family, talking about the day's events. We had to be very careful when taking our food back to our hut. Vultures waited for us and would swoop down to grab any food they could from our dishes. Occasionally, the vultures would manage to steal something. One day I was playing a game outside while holding a slice of bread with marmalade on in. I thought I could outsmart the vulture and be outside playing and still enjoy my snack. Mama had warned, "Don't go outside while eating the bread – the vultures are also hungry." I had replied, "I will be very careful." Unexpectedly, with lightning speed, a vulture grabbed the food out of my hand and flew away, my hand left scratched and bleeding, my snack gone. Mama had to disinfect the deep gash and put a bandage on it. She repeated, "Vultures are very fast, and they have perfect vision," a bit of wisdom to live by in the bush. I learned my lesson – the vultures with their keen eyesight were faster and smarter than I.

An unfortunate choice when selecting a location for hut construction could mean ongoing problems for the residents. The cause of this potential distress was…termites. They gnawed on carpets, shoes, clothes, et cetera, and built freestanding mud structures that were sturdy and required a lot of effort to destroy. Each morning, we would discover a new mound, and it was hard to win the war against millions of termites. The mounds meant that there was a colony under the hut, and the termites were almost impossible to purge. It was a constant struggle because the remedies used to exterminate proved to be futile. Termites were one more challenge and annoyance about life in the wild.

Tiny ants. Who could imagine the havoc these tiny pests could create? Millions of them invaded the hut and crawled all over the bed or sleeping person. Our defense was a spray can with a mixture of kerosene and pyrethrum. Most camp residents fought a daily battle with these tiny ants.

I hoped to have the privilege of owning a pet monkey. Whenever I saw a native boy with a cute monkey in a wicker cage, I would ask how much he would sell it for. The answer was always "five schillings." I would always ask him to wait while I checked with my mother. Mama demanded to know the purpose for the money. While I continued to plead, she would try to reason with me. She explained, "We live in a one-room hut and don't have the facilities to care for a pet that needs food suited for his health and room to climb." Grudgingly, I accepted the explanation until the next time…when I saw another cute monkey in a wicker cage for sale. Oh, what a pity! One more unrealized dream, and I felt sad for our circumstances.

However, I could have an angora kitten as a pet. My friend's cat had just had kittens. I fell in love with their blue eyes. I was allowed to bring one home to show my mother. We ended up keeping the cat. We called him Tiger because he looked and often behaved like one. He stayed in the hut and sometimes caught small creatures that he would proudly show to us. It petrified my mother. Shortly before we left the camp, he went out for a stroll and never came back. We missed him, but we knew that soon we would have to leave him anyway because the camp was slated to close, and we would be relocating.

HAZARDS OF LIFE
IN KIDUGALA

CAMP KIDUGALA WAS divided into two sections. The river flowed through the middle of the camp. We had no washing machines. The mothers typically did the family's laundry in the river, pounding the clothes on rocks or sharing a washboard to rub the dirt out – the way it had been done for centuries. This was not an easy task. After washing, the clothes were dried outside on a clothesline. Every piece of clothing had to be ironed because flies laid eggs on them. Then as we wore the clothes, the flies would hatch and worms would burrow under the skin, creating a lump that required medical attention to be removed. I had a pimple on my check that was red and getting bigger each day. Mama decided that the lump should be checked by the doctor. It turned out to be a worm, which the doctor easily removed. The doctor instructed all the camp residents to make certain to iron each and every piece of clothing worn, including towels. Since there was no electricity, the iron had to be heated on warm coals and then used to disinfect the clothes as well as smooth out wrinkles.

The camp doctor also told us to carefully check our feet every evening to see if any pesky microscopic sand fleas or jiggers had gnawed their way into the toes or the heels of exposed feet, penetrating deep into the flesh. They would deposit a membrane of eggs under the skin. In a few days, the sand fleas would hatch and cause an infection or gangrene. The camp residents were horrified when Mrs. Czerwonka died of gangrene caused by the sand fleas.

Every evening, we needed to bring home warm water from the dining area. Henia would begin her evening ritual, bringing water and gathering her things to wash up before bed. I would jump into the warm water she had brought home and quickly wash before Henia had a chance to do so. She would return to the wash basin to find the water already dirty and become angry with me for being too lazy to fetch my own clean water. It took us awhile to adjust to our life in camp Kidugala. We then developed a routine and followed activities according to a designated schedule.

During the rainy season, thunder roared like great cannons and there were blinding flashes of lightning. Lightning would often strike an outcropping of rocks near the camp, then the dark sky would open and torrents of rain would pound the huts and earth. Violent storms and frequent loud thunder would shake the hut. The bolts of lightning reverberated through the huts and ground when it struck close by. During one such storm, the house next door was struck by lightning. The roof began to burn despite of the heavy rain. Henia and I were panic-stricken. We ran outside and stood in the pouring rain, crying and paralyzed with fear. Relief washed over us when we saw Mama hurrying toward us from work. "Why aren't you carrying our bedding out to the neighbor's house?" she asked. The wind was blowing in the direction of our house, and flames had already ignited another roof. We sprang into action, grabbing items from our hut and running to a neighbor's house to leave them there for safe keeping. I ran into the house, grabbed a small suitcase of books, scooped up my pet cat and began to run out. My mother exclaimed, "Drop the cat! He will save himself! Drop the books and grab some bedding!" She explained, "Once the thatched roof collapses, the danger to our house will pass because the wind will not carry burning embers to ignite another roof." After about ten minutes, the roof collapsed, and we gave a sigh of relief because the danger had passed. Thank God, the worst was over. Our lives' necessities were safe. Mama and Henia teased me for a long time, saying that I wasn't much help in an emergency because my priorities were flawed. I was seven years old. Give me credit for trying to help!

One afternoon, a group of us were playing near our home. We played simple games like softball, hopscotch, and jump rope. Henia and Babcia were in the hut, and Mama was working. Suddenly, we heard loud noises and an animated discussion concerning the danger posed by a huge snake. The reason for the chatter was a boa constrictor resting in the eucalyptus tree near the church. My friends and I became curious and rushed in the direction of the church. A large group of people were gathered a few feet from the tree, making spirited comments. One young African, who worked in our camp, lived in the nearby village, and spoke some Polish, explained that the snake had swallowed a goat and was now resting in the tree. A big bump was plainly visible on his body. The snake was very long. Its head was resting in the fork of the tree, and a few feet of its body hung loosely from a large branch. A camp policeman came to investigate and said that plans were being made to shoot the boa before it digested the goat and started to look for its next victim. For a few days, the main topics of discussion were boa constrictors and how they can camouflage themselves in the trees, ready to pounce, and the other inherent dangers in our lives in the African bush.

Often, warnings were posted on a bulletin board near the church and on a freestanding message structure near the kitchen. The notices warned the reader not to venture too far from camp because wild animals had been sighted nearby. Serious warnings were issued to camp residents routinely, prohibiting them from venturing outside the camp periphery, especially at sunset. One day, such a warning was posted. A lion's presence had been confirmed by paw prints near the river. We realized that after dinner Babcia and a friend had gone for a stroll outside the camp gate. That evening the three of us – Mama, Henia and I, as well as the daughter of Babcia's friend – stood anxiously by the gate awaiting the return of the two dear, older women. When they came into view, we rushed toward them, relieved to see them. We hurried home as dusk was enveloping the camp, grateful that everyone was safe. The camp often buzzed with stories of lions roaming nearby. Lion attacks were the one of the main topics of excitement, with stories and details repeated.

One Sunday afternoon, while inside observing "tropical hours," we suddenly heard drum beating, screams and wailing. We ran outside to hear that a lion had killed a native mother with her baby tied to her back. She had been outside working in the maize patch. People ran down the path leading to the village. My seven-year-old mind whispered, "That's worth investigating," so I joined the group and ran to the village. Henia ran out of the house, calling after me, but I was already too far down the path. Arriving at the village, I saw a body wrapped in a straw mat. I continued to hear wailing, drum beating and loud chanting. The village was in mourning, and they expressed their grief loudly. The villagers were chanting "*Bibi Mtoto,*" which means "baby" and "mother" in Swahili, over and over for a long time. The adults urged us to go back to our huts before darkness fell. Lion sightings continued to be reported. Paw prints were seen near the river, and plans were made to trap and kill the lion before someone in our community was attacked. The camp policemen and several men from the camp devised various ways to trap the intruder. They constructed a tree house and spent three nights ready to act when the lion appeared. A small animal was tied to a nearby tree to entice the lion. However, nothing came of these plans, and they complained that they had spent three sleepless nights to no avail. After a time, the chatter about the lion died down, and regular activities resumed. About a month later, the camp residents were enjoying a quiet dinner time when there was a great racket. Loud drum beating, tin jingling, and chanting sounds were heard as a group of Africans approached the center of the camp. People emerged from their homes, frightened by this bedlam. A strange scene unfolded. A large group of Africans dressed in colorful strange-looking attire entered the square. A dead lion was tied to a long pole carried on the shoulders of two warriors. Others in the group performed a rhythmic dance. Those dancing had tins tied to their ankles, and the jingling noise continued. They chanted "*Hatari sana simba,*" which means "very dangerous lion." They dropped the lion in the middle of the square. Then the witch doctor, with his painted face and strange headgear, stepped forward, and the chanting stopped. There was complete silence, only the pounding of our fast-beating hearts in our chests. Everyone felt anxious. The witch doctor jumped and made strange noises while chanting. Then he took a spear and plunged it into the lion. The Africans were certain that he had the power to put a spell on all the lions in the area. This continued for a time, and then, with the witch doctor at the head of the throng, they left the camp. Everyone spoke about the unusual ritual for many days. Maybe it was a coincidence or the power of the witch doctor, but we were never bothered by lions again. It seemed that the "Lion Kingdom" label for Camp Kidugala was accurate.

Shortly after the lion incident, an African who worked in the camp taught the children the following poem. He was very pleased to hear us reciting the poem as we jumped rope or played outside. I can still recall it:

"Moja bili tatu	"One, two, three
Simba nakula kyatu	Lion ate shoes
Memsap naliya	Lady cried
Simba naki-mbiya	Lion ran away
Moja bili tatu"	One, two, three"

A few other phrases in Swahili that we learned and used, in addition to being able to count to fifty, were:

Jambo	-	Hello, good morning, or how are you?
Mzuri kawisa	-	I'm well
Kwenda zako	-	Go away
Siafu	-	Tiny ants
Kwaheri Africa	-	Goodbye, Africa
Kwaheri rafiki	-	Goodbye, friends
Muzuri sana	-	Very good
Nidyo kweli	-	It's true

MORE SADNESS

WHEN OUR LIVES had finally settled into a routine, we were able to adjust to most of the challenges faced as residents of the African bush: night noises, malaria, parasites, tropical scorching sun, wildlife, carving a community from the jungle. Then another jolt, not from the sky but like thunder, filled us with agonizing sorrow. This sudden event had a long-lasting effect on our emotions and futures, and our hearts. Our beloved Babcia was called by God to her eternal rest on March 17, 1946.

Babcia's gall bladder surgery in Persia had not been performed properly. It left an opening in her abdomen that would not heal. The incision constantly drained and needed daily attention. She wore a dressing around her waist that frequently needed to be changed and adjusted. She died from these complications and most likely an infection. We were fortunate to have the services of Father Maciaszek. At Mama's request, Henia and I summoned the priest, and he arrived in time to bless Babcia and administer Last Rites.

We had hoped to enjoy our more stable life in Africa together for a few years. God's perception was different. He wanted to give Babcia everlasting peace and reward her sooner than we had hoped, and definitely before we were ready to let her go. She was laid to rest in a consecrated cemetery where selfless and dedicated nuns, priests and missionaries were already buried.

Many years before our arrival, Camp Kidugala had been a German mission. In the 1920s, there had been a revolt by the native African people against the Christian teaching and lifestyles under the slogan "Africa for Africans." Many missionaries were killed. The church was destroyed, except for the foundation, which was later restored by the Polish people. This new church was where we worshipped and where fervent prayers for peace, the safe return of our loved ones, and world harmony were sent heavenward.

Babcia was a very important member of our family, helping in whatever way possible to make our lives easier. Mama had to work, so it was Babcia who watched over Henia and me when we came home from school. I needed supervision because I was only six years old. I can still hear her saying, "First homework, then play," or warning, "Your mother needs to hear this and deal with you." As I think back decades later, I understand that in our primitive circumstances, nothing was easy. For example, one day, Babcia bought corn from an African and walked some distance to the communal kitchen to make a snack for us when we came home from school. I was too young to fully appreciate the love that motivated her actions. Babcia refused to allow me to play, and my friends were waiting outside. She said, "Eat the corn and do your homework." When she asked how the corn tasted, I answered, "It's hard and gray." Her feelings were hurt, and she said that my response was inappropriate. As an adult, I regret making that remark to my dear, kind-hearted Babcia, but it is too late to take back the words. However, as a mother, I believe that she would understand that these were just the words of a young child.

We were crushed by Babcia's death – so much pain in our lives. Babcia had prayed and hoped that the four of her children in Communist Poland would survive the fury of war. Unfortunately, it was only two months after she passed away that they were located by the Red Cross. Ciocia Stenia, Ciocia Aniela and Wujek Jozek were alive. Her oldest son, Stanislaw, was the only one of Babcia's eleven children killed during the war. He had been murdered by his Ukrainian neighbors, incited by the Soviets to violence. We were disappointed that Babcia had not received the information about her children while she was alive. But truly, Babcia's arrival in heaven had most likely immediately revealed to her what we now knew. I was very sad that my Babcia wasn't there when I received my First Holy Communion. The celebration was tempered by her absence. I will, for the rest of my life, continue to try to emulate Babcia's and my mother's high ideals and deep faith. That is the least that I can do.

Remarkably, Babcia's remaining children survived the war, and they were all devastated by her death. Her sons experienced deep heartache and wrote of their grief. Her youngest son, Wujek Ludwik, wrote that he would often find an isolated place to grieve and cry in solitude.

In June 1946, a message over the radio resonated with the residents of Kidugala. The British government was wrestling with the serious dilemma of how to reunite the Polish army veterans in Europe with their families in East Africa and India. Demobilization of the Second Polish Corp and their transfer to the United Kingdom had begun. To facilitate the complicated process, the Resettlement Corps was created. The main purpose was to teach the veterans and their families English and other skills that would help with their reintegration into civilian life. This was a monumental task because of the large number of people and the enormous distances involved. To achieve this goal, a lot of money and resources were needed, along with time to implement and finalize the process. Money from the Polish gold bullion that had been transferred to England for safekeeping before World War II was used for the soldiers' and their families' expenses.

This radio message caused the residents of the camp great anxiety – more travel, more uncertainty. But we were grateful to the British government for launching this course of action. Later, we learned that the Allied countries were working with the British government, and a timeline estimated that it would take two years to accomplish everything. Camp Kidugala buzzed with anticipation and the news that the settlement would be closing. We would be relocating to Ifunda, another camp closer to the port from which we would sail to Europe.

When actual liquidation of the camp began, the segregation of families commenced. We were separated into two groups, the women and children who were being reunited and those who, sadly, had lost their loved ones and no longer had anyone with whom to be reunited. Families to be reunited were heading to England. The Kidugala residents who had no one with whom to reunite could chose to immigrate to countries like New Zealand, Australia, or other countries willing to accept them. These families signed a two-year contract agreeing to work to repay any expenses. Families could also choose to return to Poland. A few families decided to take a chance and return to Poland under a Communist regime. As families were separated according to their final destinations, many were transferred temporarily to other camps. Since we would be reuniting with my father in England, we were relocated to Ifunda.

As we packed to leave the safety of Kidugala, we experienced conflicting sentiments, including nostalgia and frustration. Our emotions were intense because the ties and friendships that had evolved here were strong. We had bonded due to our shared traumatic experiences – two years of Siberian hell, the stress of family members fighting for world peace, daily exposure to danger and the always present uncertainty of our future. We bid goodbye to dear friends with whom we had shared bitter, sweet and everyday struggles and memories for three years. We had survived this isolated life as a community, carving out an oasis deep in the bush, in the middle of Neverland. We were a family of one thousand individuals of various ages and faiths – Roman Catholic, Jewish, and Orthodox. Kidugala was where deep wounds began to heal, where we came face-to-face with our reality, where we helped each other survive and thrive. Together, we had created a harmonious environment full of positive energy with activities where our children's evolution was of the utmost importance. As I grow older and ponder the years spent in East Africa, I am astonished that these young mothers possessed the intellectual acumen and talent to create an environment that fostered a congenial atmosphere for their children with the extremely limited resources that were available in such primitive circumstances. Their proverbial "making something out of nothing" was close to genius. I am certain that if it were possible to poll those who had spent part of their formative years in that isolated but enriched environment, we would find that they became high achievers, living by high ideals. This was a "controlled" niche where the adage "it takes a village to raise a child" proved to be a fact.

Our hearts were heavy with sadness at the thought of leaving Babcia's grave in Kidugala. We would no longer be able to visit her resting place, light a votive candle and maintain the grave site. No one in their wildest nightmare could have foreseen that Babcia's final resting place would be a tiny spot on the "Dark Continent," a remote location that even decades later is difficult to find on the map.

Babcia's resting place is extremely remote even today, but not un-reachable. I am the only living family member who knew my Babcia and was lovingly cared for as a child by her. It is my hope to be able to, one last time, light a votive candle and say prayers in our native language beside her grave. Precisely because she is so far away from her precious homeland, that we are planning a journey to accom-plish this. Three generations of my family will travel to Kidugala in honor of her iconic spirit, life and memory, still dear to us over sev-enty years later.

My beloved Babcia, Maria. Tehran 1942/43.

Babcia's resting place in the cemetery near the church in Kidugala, Tanzania,
March 17, 1946.

CAMP IFUNDA

IN APRIL 1947, we left for the new settlement. It was the third camp in our almost five-year sojourn in East Africa. Trucks arrived, and we again traveled on corrugated, sometimes muddy, roads to Ifunda. As we traveled through the countryside, we were mesmerized by exotic sights that almost took our breath away. The termite-created structures, the red clay, the skittish gazelles hopping gracefully into the air, herds of zebras looking in our direction flicking their tails, ostriches galloping away from the noise of the trucks, giraffes walking along, and the occasional lion family resting in the shade of the baobab tree. We admired the unique kaleidoscope of shapes, colors and sights of this vast wilderness. After many hours in the truck, we arrived at a new camp and faced the uncertainty of meeting new people, forming new friendships, registering in a new school and becoming accustomed to new surroundings.

Shortly after we moved to Ifunda, on my way home from school, I heard the yelling and jeering of a group of boys. They were throwing rocks at a long-legged crane. I intervened and threatened to tell their mothers about the incident. The boys ran away. As I turned, the crane followed me home. I gave him water and food and he became our pet. We called him Maciek. Every morning Maciek came and chirped by the door. We continued to supplement his diet. We gave him seeds, and he would come into our hut to drink water from a pail that we placed near the door for him. At dusk, he would leave, and we didn't know where he stayed overnight. Each morning, he would be by the door again. When we went somewhere, Maciek followed right behind. He would follow me to school and then would walk back to our hut while I was in class. Maciek would be waiting for me when school was over and then follow me wherever I went.

At times, I had to sneak away without him noticing and following. One Sunday, he followed us all the way to church and refused to listen when I told him to go back and wait for us by our hut. While Mass begun, Maciek walked right into the church and proceeded down the center aisle looking for us. I had to escort him outside. Maciek then patiently waited outside until the service ended and walked home with us.

A short time later, Mama had to stay at the hospital for a few days for treatment. Henia went to visit her, and Maciek followed right behind. The next morning, while Henia and I were at school, Mama heard Maciek chirping by the hospital door. He was such a smart bird. He had found his way back to the hospital to visit her. It just so happened, Mama was going to be discharged that day. When Henia came to help Mama home, Maciek walked with them. My mother would always happily recall how Maciek escorted them home. It was uncanny that this wild bird became so attached to us. He seemed to know where we were and to always look after us. A reporter came and filmed us with Maciek. Our special relationship was supposed to have made the news reels in Europe!

We lived at Camp Ifunda for a year and a half. One day, the adults were urged to attend a meeting that concerned all of us at the camp. After attending the meeting, Mama returned home with concern visible on her face. We would be relocating again. Once again, there were emotional moments full of tears and goodbyes that reverberated over the recesses of the African wilderness. This, however, was truly our final goodbye. We were bidding, "Kawari Ifunda" ("Goodbye, Ifunda").

Needless to say, we were heartbroken at the thought of leaving Maciek behind when it was time to go. On the day of our departure, we were wearing slacks, and he noticed the change in our apparel, eyeing us suspiciously and quizzically. Before we boarded our truck, we gave him hugs and kissed his head. We cried as the trucks drove away. We loved him dearly. We hoped that either someone would adopt him or that he would be able to fend for himself.

In March 1948, we traveled to the port city of Mombasa, Kenya. Our ship would not arrive for three weeks. We were placed in an ex-military camp near the beach. The time in port was advantageous and enjoyable for us. Each morning after breakfast, we headed to the beach and spent many hours breathing the fresh ocean air, collecting specimens that we found on the sand and swimming. Occasionally, we went on a guided tour of Mombasa. We believed that most likely we would not return to this far-flung part of the world. Mama bought several souvenirs as mementos. With limited resources and by being frugal, we purchased ebony carvings – of a native man and woman, a giraffe and a crane, like Maciek. To this day, these mementos remain in our family.

On March 19, 1946, the prime minister of Great Britain, C. R. Attlee, informed General Anders that Polish forces had completed their transfer to Britain and were demobilized. Families from Africa and India were on their way to being reunited in England. The war had ended, the military camps in Britain were empty, and the British government made these ex-military and air force camps available to the Polish veterans and their families. These camps were now called hostels and would serve as temporary housing for the Polish exiles.

On June 8, 1946, a victory parade was joyfully held in London, England. In spite of their participation in the war effort, the Polish troops were not invited to take part in the parade. The British were afraid of Stalin's reaction if they invited the Poles. Poland was un-der Communist rule, and Stalin's feelings were to be considered. The Polish troops were deeply wounded by this cruel snub and lack of consideration for their feelings and sacrifices. They had given their all in battle, losing friends and relatives, and the world leaders inflicted yet another wound by denying them the honor of participating in the victory parade. Apparently, the world had a very short memory. The Polish army was the fourth largest fighting force in the Allied alliance. The spineless leaders, by my judgment, were not guided by principle but by fear. Shame on them.

Henia, holding Maciek, standing with friends, 1946.

Krysia, standing far right, and friends with Maciek, 1947.

Henia touching Maciek. Mama standing to the right of Maciek, with friends..

ENGLAND

THE VOYAGE TO England took three weeks. We sailed on the *Carnarvon Castle*, part of the Union-Castle Mail Steamship Company Limited. It was a difficult journey because of the stifling heat and cabins without air-conditioning. We spent most of our time on deck. At the start of our trip, we again had to practice evacuation procedures. They were boring and time-consuming sessions. We realized, however, that it was better to be safe than sorry, so everyone participated. The Indian Ocean was calm. The water was so deep that it looked black. The first port where we stopped to refuel and take on fresh supplies was Aden, Yemen. Then we journeyed north on the Red Sea, still uncomfortable due to the extreme heat. The children were disappointed that the water was in fact not red in the Red Sea, but aqua and calm.

Several days later, we sailed through the Suez Canal. We had to sail slowly because of the depth of the canal. Periodically, silt at the bottom of the canal needed to be removed because it became too shallow for ships to pass. Arab merchants, in small boats, sailed alongside, calling out to us on deck. They displayed their wares and tried to entice us into buying their goods, which included rugs, dried fruit, jewelry and clothing. This was a comical activity. Pantomime and sign language were used when haggling over the price of the item. When a purchase was agreed upon, the item was hoisted in a basket up to a person on deck and money was sent down. Trust was involved here. The yelling and trying to make a sale went on the entire length of the canal.

Upon reaching Port Said (Bur Said), Egypt, the ship needed to again stop for refueling and additional supplies. We next sailed upon the Mediterranean Sea. It was a beautiful blue-green color reflecting streams of sunlight. We crossed almost the entire width of the Mediterranean Sea. As we headed out into the Atlantic Ocean, we passed Gibraltar. Everyone came out on deck, and we prayed as a group and sang the Polish national anthem. This was our heartfelt tribute to the great General Wladyslaw Sikorski because this was the very spot where he had perished in an airplane crash. We considered him our savior because he had been the one who negotiated with Stalin and began the process of organizing the Polish army on Soviet soil. *"Czesc jego pamieci!"* "We salute you!" we all called out.

We completed our voyage a few days later, docking in Southampton, England. It was May 4, 1948. From the port, we were transported to several transit hostels, first to Possingworth West, then to Sussex, south of London, which had been vacated by the British army, and then to Barron's Cross. We were quarantined for two weeks, waiting to obtain necessary documents. We were very anxious to be reunited with our father.

I feel a deep, sincere gratitude to the two gallant patriots – Colonel Ignacy Matuszewski and Major Henryk Floyar Rajchman – who transported the Polish gold to England. The bullion was used to provide for us. We were without a country, but we were not a charity case, because of the Polish gold reserve. In 2015, their remains, as expressed in their wills, were returned to Poland from the United States. Poland did not forget its debt to these men. They were buried with full military honors among other heroes from decades' past. I salute these courageous men. *Wieczne wam odpoczywanie* – "rest in peace."

Regardless of the duration of our stay in any hostel, school was a priority and immediately organized. Classes were styled after the traditional one-room schoolhouse. Young people were not left at loose ends, but constantly involved in learning.

One day, as three friends and I were coming home from school, I saw my mother and a man waiting for us. As we approached, Mama asked the man if he could pick his daughter out from the group. He said that he was not sure which one of the four was his daughter. Sadness was visible on Tata's face and emotion raw in his voice. When my father had left for basic training and military service, I was only five years old, and now I was eleven. He had missed many milestones in our lives. Our family reunion was so joyful and emotional because we had doubted that such a reunion was possible and always worried if we would ever be a family again.

To allow the newly reunited families to adjust to the British way of life, the British government made available now vacant army and air force camps as housing. With buildings destroyed, it was difficult to find housing for so many. The empty hostels were available for a reasonable price to the Polish exiles. This would give us time and space to become reacquainted, make decisions and acclimate to the new country, expectations and climate. Another reason to allow Polish veterans to live in the hostels was to give them time to learn the language and, in some cases, a trade or to expand their education. Various courses were offered. The hostels were also cultural and religious centers. Lectures, concerts and movies were shown, and on weekends, dances and social events were held. Many of the young people socialized, married and were assimilated into the British population.

My family lived in three hostels. First was Rednal, located near Oswestry in Shropshire about one hundred kilometers from Chester. We lived in army barracks and received two meals a day prepared in the communal kitchen. The barrack had only one or two rooms with minimal pieces of furniture. We warmed our food on electric hot plates. We had no refrigerators or stoves in the barrack. The next was Oulton Park, also near Chester. When that hostel closed, we moved to East Moor near Sutton-on-Forest about ten kilometers from the historic city of York. Our site was at the very end of the camp. There were trees and dense groves between each of the home sites. Several families lived at each site. Bathrooms, sinks, and laundry facilities were communal. They were set a distance away from the living quarters. To use the bathroom or shower, we had to go to these separate facilities. I was often afraid to walk to our site because we were the last trail, and it was forested and dark. My imagination would run wild. My friends would turn off the main path to their sites, and I would be alone for the last stretch. Often, I would ask my father or sister to walk the trail with me, especially when it was dark. If they would not walk, then I would ask that they at least stand outside, midway between our barrack and facilities, to watch me as I ran safely to the main path or to the bathroom before bedtime.

Living in East Moor gave us a chance to become acclimated to a regular lifestyle where we made our own decisions. Generally, hostels were situated near large cities. The farmlands nearby reminded the Polish residents of their previous lives. One other advantage of the hostels was that they were relatively inexpensive. When my father was discharged from the Resettlement Corps, he found employment in construction outside the city of York and rode his bike to work, regardless of the weather. Tata earned nine pounds a week. Henia rode the bus to work at the Roundtree Chocolate factory. I went to school. Mama, along with other women from the hostel, occasionally worked for local farmers as dayworkers to supplement our meager income. She would pick potatoes or vegetables. They were paid at the end of each day. Several times, my friend Alina and I would also go to pick potatoes. We had a plan to earn money with specific luxuries in mind, first and foremost, a bicycle.

When I could, I borrowed my father's bicycle to get around. It was, however, too big for me. I could not straddle the center bar and had to put my leg underneath the bar to ride. My legs were bruised from hitting the bar, and I was constantly falling off the bike. At one point, Tata said that if I had any more bruises on my legs, I would not be allowed to leave the house. East Moor Hostel was located near an abandoned airstrip. My friend and I would meet at one end whenever we could borrow a bicycle to ride up and down the runway for fun. Eventually, I was the proud owner of my own bike. I was overjoyed and happily rode everywhere.

All our food was purchased with ration cards. We were allowed one egg per person per week and had to travel to York for most items. Mama had a plan. She went to town and bought baby chicks. We kept them in a cardboard box with a light above to keep them warm.

Once they were big enough, my father made a chicken coop behind the barrack, and the chickens had free range. We could have eggs regularly and meat from time to time. One chick was a runt. He was always cold, and whenever my mother came out to feed the chicks, he would run over and stand on her foot. Mama would put the chick inside her jacket to keep him warm as she worked outside. Even when he grew up to be a healthy rooster, he would still be the first one to run up to the fence and greet her. The rooster always remembered and would still try to stand on her foot.

My friend Alina's parents also raised chickens. One day they went to a wedding and told us, because we were playing together, to make sure the chickens were in the coop before dark. We were busy playing, and suddenly darkness was upon us. We had forgotten about the chickens. Chickens cannot see in the dark. Full of trepidation, we began to frantically search for the chickens that were not in the coop, fearing that they would be eaten by wild animals during the night. We kept count each time we found another chicken roosting for the night under a bush, taking them back to the coop. We were one chicken short! Alina didn't want to be punished for losing a precious chicken and for failing in her responsibility. We again looked under every bush. With great relief, we found the last chicken some distance from the coop, already roosting for the night. All were safely returned to the coup before anyone was the wiser.

When I was twelve years old, I prevailed upon my parents to allow me to go to boarding school. Many of my friends were making similar plans. They agreed, and after proper documents were completed, I went to Diddington, two hundred miles from our hostel. The school was located about one hundred kilometers outside of London. The students lived in a vacant army hospital consisting of a series of Quonset barracks. Each looked like half of a barrel lying on its side. Twenty girls lived in each barrack. In addition to schoolwork, we had to do our own housekeeping, clean the classrooms, and make sure that the two metal stoves that provided heat for the barrack always had coal. All the chores were done on a rotating basis. We ate all three meals in a mess hall. Classes were held from 8:00 a.m. to 5:00 p.m. We studied and did homework from 7:00 p.m. to 9:00 p.m. It was lights out at 10:00 p.m. The instruction was in Polish with English as a second language. We communicated in Polish, as we had always done. I often wrote letters to my parents. We didn't have phones, and I came home only at Christmas and for the summer months.

One incident at school had a traumatic effect on me. The students in my class and I were treated to a culturally enriching activity. We went on a class trip to London. Our itinerary included visits to the Tower of London, Trafalgar Square, museums, Buckingham Palace and more. We slept on sleeping bags at a YWCA. We took a train to London and used public transportation to move about the city. After breakfast, our group waited for a double-decker bus to take us to the Tower of London. When the bus arrived, all my classmates found seats on the lower level. I sat on the upper lever and had a clear view of the London sites. When the bus arrived at its final destination, the driver found me all alone in a seat on the upper level admiring the view and the pedestrians. My classmates and the teacher had disembarked and left me on the bus. The bus driver was very kind and understanding. It was difficult for the driver to communicate with me because of my limited ability to speak English. He looked kindly at the thirteen-year-old girl wearing a school uniform – navy-blue blazer and skirt, white blouse, braids and a beret with the initials CFH, Frederic Chopin, the initials of my school. He flagged down a London bobby, a policeman, for help. I don't know how, but they delivered me safely to the YWCA where my classmates had returned full of excitement after their visit to the Tower of London. I was happy to rejoin my group even though I didn't see the tower. I imagine the teacher who chaperoned our group failed in her responsibility to check if all her charges were together. Nonetheless, this adventure ended well and is my very memorable London trip experience in 1951, more than half a century ago.

Meanwhile, Mama, Tata and Henia continued life at East Moor. It was a mini-country in exile. My parents were cognizant that it was only a temporary residence and that decisions pertaining to our future would soon need to be put into motion. Where to proceed to next?

Reunited at Barrons Cross. Family picture 1948.

Family picture with Uncle Bronek on the left 1949.

Henia feeding the chickens. East Moor 1950.

Chick on Krysia's lap, Henia standing. East Moor 1950.

Krysia riding her bicycle around East Moor.

Krysia on a motorcycle at her boarding school in Diddington.
Student barracks in the background.

Polish Folk Dancing at Diddington School. Krysia on the left.

Krysia, at left, with a friend in Trafalgar Square on a school trip, 1951

THE UNITED STATES
OF AMERICA

OUR HOPES AND aspirations were tied to the national ones. The Yalta Treaty diminished the hope that we would be able to return to a free Poland at the end of the war. We realized how little trust one can place in international treaties and promises.

In February 11, 1945, at the Yalta Conference held in Yalta, Crimea, the world's three most powerful leaders – President of the United States Franklin D. Roosevelt, Prime Minister of Britain Winston Churchill, and Chairman of the Soviet Union Joseph Stalin – signed the Yalta Treaty. This was a treacherous agreement for Poland because it reconfigured the Polish border. These leaders signed away to the Soviets 20 percent of the Polish Eastern Territories. An American diplomat, Bliss Land, who was at the Yalta Conference, wrote a moving account of this meeting in a book titled, *I Saw Poland Betrayed*. A British historian, Norman Davis, condemned the treaty as "handing the devastated country of Poland to the Soviets on a silver platter." These two principled men recognized and called out this unfair agreement. The weak-minded Western statesmen were duped by Stalin, the cruel tyrant. The sacrifices made by the valiant Polish troops to secure the freedom of Britain and the world were dismissed as of little value, not worthy of consideration. The highly esteemed Roosevelt and Churchill proved to be short-sighted and ignorant, lacking vision of the future and did not realize that the sadistic dictator Stalin would not be easily appeased. Just by their signatures, they endangered and complicated the lives of many generations. Their misjudged decisions had far-reaching consequences.

The eastern territories of Poland had been home to many generations of my family and many of the soldiers who sacrificed their lives in World War II. Presently, Halicz, where I was born, is part of the Ukraine. One signature of the weak-minded leaders made these drastic transformations, affecting millions whose birthplace is now in a different country.

In 1952, I received a letter from my parents instructing me to return home. We were immigrating to the United States. In 1950, the U.S. Congress passed a resolution allowing eighteen thousand veterans and their families to immigrate to the United States if they had a sponsor. At that time, each ethnic group had a quota. The sponsor would help them find a job and housing, so these immigrants would not be a burden to the U.S. government. The many Polish Americans who volunteered to sponsor the new arrivals should be recognized. In most cases, they sponsored total strangers. We knew a family from the hostel in East Moor who had relocated to Worcester, Massachusetts. They were sponsored by their American aunt. They helped find a sponsor for us, a stranger, Mr. Konczanin.

Before we could immigrate, proper documents had to be completed. Rigorous screenings and health examinations were performed, including X-rays and bloodwork by American physicians. Once physicals were passed, an interview at an American embassy was scheduled. The Americans were worried that, God forbid, we were Communist sympathizers. The very idea was repugnant to us. We had barely survived "Communist paradise" and were cured for life from that ideology.

When all the formalities were completed, we packed our meager belongings into three suitcases. My father had $100 in his wallet for unforeseen expenses. We left East Moor by train for Southampton. We sailed from Southampton on April 9, 1952, aboard the *Queen Mary*, Cunard White Star Limited shipping line, to the New World.

However, we were heartbroken because Henia was not allowed to come with us. She was older and not considered part of the veteran's family. Also, Henia's X-ray showed a small spot on her lung. The spot turned out to be nothing, but it was enough to prevent her from initially joining us. Henia remained with a family friend in England, sharing an apartment and working in London for four years.

We arrived in New York on April 14, 1952, after five days at sea, with all our worldly possessions. We had to pay for the tickets ourselves because my parents missed the due date to apply for government assistance with the crossing. The immigration officials boarded the ship, checked our documents and allowed us to disembark at Ellis Island. We were on our own in a strange country. Although no one welcomed us as we sailed into New York harbor, the sight of Lady Liberty was nevertheless heartwarming to us. Just like millions of immigrants before us, she was the only one to greet us. The light she holds represented to us the hope for a better future where darkness is dispelled by the beacon of her flame. We took a cab to the railway station and bought tickets to Worcester, Massachusetts. We stayed for a week with our friends, and they helped my father find work and a place for us to stay.

In Worcester, we met our sponsor, Mr. Konczanin. He owned a furniture store. He was simply our sponsor – just a formality. He did not help us in any other way. Later, as a gesture of our gratitude, when we finally had our own apartment, we bought a secondhand washing machine and refrigerator from his store. Fortunately for us, my father found a job a week after our arrival. It was on the night shift at a company called Queensbury Combing Company in Auburn, Massachusetts. It paid minimum wage. The company shredded and cleaned wool, and Tata operated one of the machines. It was rather difficult to find housing. We were introduced to an older bachelor, who was kind-hearted and allowed us to move into his three-bedroom apartment. He was not home most of the time, so we shared his apartment on the second floor on Green Street in Worcester for half a year.

Mama became sick shortly after arriving in the United States and could not get out of bed. She needed medical care and a Polish-speaking doctor made a home visit and prescribed medicine. Mama couldn't even turn over in bed. I had to wait for my father to come home from work, so together we could roll her over. For a time, she couldn't even walk. As she began to recover and became slightly mobile, I would set up chairs for her to hold on to and sit on when she needed to go to the bathroom. This simple task had become too difficult. There was no diagnosis. We thought it was the stress of the past years and the worry over her oldest daughter's circumstances. Fortunately, she eventually made a full recovery.

We lived in the United States, but our life continued to be difficult. After a few months on the job, before we were able to save any substantial amount of money, my father developed pneumonia and couldn't work for a month. It was difficult to pay rent and have enough money for groceries. We asked the man from whom we were renting the house if we could be in arrears for a month or two. Luckily, he was sympathetic and agreed.

I was fifteen years old and enrolled as a freshman at St. Mary's High School, a parochial school. My twenty-five classmates had been together since kindergarten, and I was totally different. My hair in braids, speaking very little English, I felt that my classmates simply tolerated me. I accepted my situation, concentrated on getting good grades and my many responsibilities at home. Since my mother was sick and unable to leave the house, I did all the shopping, cleaning, and laundry in the bath tub because we had no washing machine at that time. This was a lot of responsibility for a fifteen-year-old in a new country, with no relatives to help make this transition smoother.

Ciocia Stenia, Wujek Jozek, and Ciocia Aniela were back in Poland. Other relatives had immigrated to Canada – Wujek Ludwik, Wujek Bronek, and my cousin Ignac who later brought over his father, Szczepan, and mother, Marcela. We were the only ones in the United States. After a year, Mama recovered and went to work as a seamstress, earning minimum wage. We were frugal, budgeted well, and could purchase a secondhand washing machine, refrigerator, and some furniture from the Salvation Army. The washing machine had a wringer to wring the clothes dry. Once, while doing the laundry, my right hand became caught in the rollers. I called for help, but no one was there to help me. Fortunately for me, the rollers released my hand, but there was a five-inch rip between my fourth and pinky fingers. Mama stopped the bleeding and bandaged my hand, but I had to walk to the doctor's office by myself, so he could stitch the rip. Fortunately, it healed well after a few days.

Several other Polish veterans' families also lived in Worcester, so we enjoyed a social life of picnics, holiday celebrations and weddings. When I turned sixteen, I found a part-time job. I worked after school and on weekends as a sales clerk at Lederman's Bakery. My parents allowed me to keep my earnings. I saved and diligently planned my purchases: a record player, a class ring, a pearl necklace – small but, for me, significant luxuries.

We were overjoyed to learn that Henia would finally be able to join us. She had completed her documents and the mandatory waiting period for immigration and passed her health screenings. She left England on October 4, 1956, sailing on the *Ile de France*, and arrived in the United States on October 12, 1956. Henia also worked at Lederman's Bakery, as a full-time sales clerk. We were happy to be all together again in a new country, hoping for a good future.

In 1957, shortly after my graduation from high school, my father suffered a heart attack. The doctor said it was not serious, but we worried about him because he was the head of our family. Tata was home on sick leave for two months. He was bored and very anxious to go back to work. He scheduled a medical appointment and had a stress test and his doctor decided that he could work as long as it was not strenuous. He happily returned to work at Queensbury. Three days later, there was a knock on the door at 2:00 a.m. A policeman delivered devastating news that Tata had suffered a massive heart attack and, despite immediate help, had died. We were crushed. He was too young to die, only fifty-five years old. His life had just become a little easier and could be enjoyed. Our future had looked brighter. My uncles, Ludwik and Bronek, came to the funeral from Canada. Only the family and a small group of friends mourned the loss of a kind, loyal family man.

After the funeral, I began work as a file clerk at Massachusetts Protective Association, an insurance firm. My duties included typing information from life insurance applications, making duplicates and filing. I earned the minimum wage of one dollar an hour. I saved as much as I could, although I also contributed to the family's general expenses, such as rent and groceries. We were frugal. I walked to and from work every day, one mile each way. The bus fare would eat away my savings, so I preferred to walk and save the fifteen cents. My goal was to eventually pursue a profession.

On June 20, 1960, we celebrated Henia's marriage to Jozef Slowikowski. Wujek Ludwik walked her down the aisle to give her away. I was Henia's maid of honor. Jozef worked in the Fafnir bearing factory, producing airplane components, in New Britain, Connecticut. A year later, on March 18, 1961, we were overjoyed to welcome their daughter, Christine, into our family.

The apartment Mama and I rented had no central heating. It had an oil-burning stove that didn't heat the apartment very well since the building was poorly constructed and drafty. We didn't have a car and walked everywhere. Wujek Jozek, who immigrated to Canada with his wife, Krysia, and two children, Adam and Basia, asked me about my career plans when we visited them in Toronto. He asked if there were possibilities for advancement within the department. My response was negative. Then he asked, "Will you be happy at this dead-end job?" He encouraged me to enroll at a community college. Finally, although feeling insecure about what I perceived to be gaps in my education, I enrolled in Worcester Junior College, and majored in business management after a three-year absence from school. I worried that I hadn't saved enough for tuition. The walk to school took me thirty minutes and was unpleasant in inclement weather. My bag full of textbooks slowed me down. I was pleasantly surprised when my grades were good, even though I continued to work as a sales clerk at the bakery on weekends. After two years, I graduated with an associate's degree in business management. I transferred to the University of Bridgeport in Bridgeport, Connecticut, where I was accepted as a business major. For an inexplicable reason, I changed my major to elementary education shortly before I registered for my courses. The dean of education accepted most my credits as electives, but I still lost twenty-five credits. To graduate as soon as possible, I enrolled in summer school. Since I attended school in another state, my expenses now included rent and living expenses. In order to defray the cost of tuition, I worked twenty hours at the music library and, on weekends, as a waitress in a family-owned restaurant. Looking back, I realize that I probably qualified for some kind of scholarship or financial assistance, but I never applied for such. I always wanted to do everything without extra help. Fortunately, despite all these responsibilities, I earned a spot on the Dean's List. I graduated with honors in 1964 from the University of Bridgeport with a bachelor's degree in elementary education.

Shortly after graduation, I applied for a teaching position in Buffalo, New York. Wujek Bronek had married a woman named Anna Miller. She was from Buffalo, and he had moved to Buffalo from Toronto, Ontario, Canada. I was hired as a third-grade teacher in a Buffalo public school. With Wujek Bronek's advice, I bought a two-family house and settled permanently in the Western New York area. My mother, sister, Henia, and three-year-old niece, Christine, came to live with me, and we helped each other. We were happy to be closer to our relatives. Most were in Toronto, a few in Sudbury: Wujek Szczepan and Ciocia Marcela; Wujek Ludwik and his wife, Daniela, with children Karen and George; Wujek Jozek and his wife, Ciocia Krysia, with children Adam and Basia; Ciocia Stenia and her second husband, Fred, and her son, Andrew; Ignac and Irena with their children, Teresa, Richard, and Mark. Toronto was only 160 kilometers away. We visited them often and sometimes spent holidays together. The entire family thrived and grew. We celebrated weddings and welcomed new babies.

I took graduate classes at Buffalo State College in the summer and evenings. I received a master's degree in elementary education and then passed multiple examinations to obtain my permanent teaching certification in New York State. I worked hard, enjoyed my profession, and have always been proud to be a teacher.

Szczecin

Gdańsk

Wilno

Baranowicze

Białystok

Poznań

Brześć

WARSZAWA

1947
border

Łódź

Wrocław

Lublin

Curzon
line "B"

Kraków

Lwów

Halicz

Stanisławów

annexed by
Poland in 1945

annexed by
Soviet Union in 1945

THE CURZON LINE

Map of pre- and post-World War II Poland.

Our first family photo after Henia arrived in the United States, 1956.

Mama and Tata having a picnic by the lake near Worcester, MA.

Mama and Krysia at the cemetery.

Henia's wedding to Jozek Slowikowski, June 18, 1960.

Henia and Jozek's wedding. Krysia at left, Ludwik, at the right.

Krysia graduating from Buffalo State College with her
Masters in Elementary Education, 1968.

BABCIA'S CHILDREN

MARIA GRZESLO, MY Babcia, was an idealist. She was very progressive in her vision and the prospects of her children. In prewar Poland, primary education was free, but secondary education was not. After her husband, Jan, passed away, Maria became responsible for the family. A loving matriarch, she was deeply concerned and involved in providing advantages for her children. Babcia decided that her children needed to pursue higher education. To accomplish this, she arranged to sell some of their valuable farmland. This must have been quite stressful for a landowner whose family's livelihood was directly tied to the land. She had to conceive and execute a meticulous strategy to send Bronek to study and apprentice as a grocer, Jozek to study agronomy, Stenia to study clothing design, and Ludwik to study business.

I'd now like to share some special memories and provide some insight into each of Babcia's children, my dear *Ciocias* and *Wujeks*. These remarkable souls were extremely humble people, inclined to judge themselves as unexceptional and not worthy of admiration or accolades. I am the last family member who experienced many of these joyful and painful events, so I feel obligated to share some perceptions gained over the decades. Reflection upon these incredible people over time has provided me with a panoramic view. Despite challenges dealt by fate, these individuals consistently exhibited integrity, spirituality, resilience, morality, and a work ethic imbued in them by Babcia, as well as other talents that are too many to list.

Stanislaw – Estimated Year of Birth 1901, Died 1940

Stanislaw, the oldest son, was a hardworking landowner with a wife, Stefa, and three small children – Tadeusz (Tadek), Eugenia (Genia), and Stanislaw. His family was inexplicably omitted from the list of the deportees to Siberia. He remained in Poland and was stoned to death at the age of thirty-nine when taking a short-cut through a Ukrainian village to seek a midwife for his pregnant wife. Sadly, the baby was born after he was murdered, and Stefa named the baby boy Stanislaw, after his father. Fortunately, Babcia never learned of her son's untimely and horrific death because, at the time, we were in Siberia, completely cut off from the outside world. It was only after Babcia's death that the Red Cross located our family behind the Iron Curtain, Communist-controlled Poland, and we were able to contact Stanislaw's family. Tadeusz, Genia and Stanislaw, along with their families, still live outside Wroclaw, Poland. They are successful professionals.

Karolina (Bystryk) – Estimated Year of Birth 1903, Estimated Death 1926

Karolina, the oldest daughter, was a housewife who died at the age of twenty-one from complications of childbirth. Her infant daughter passed away a few weeks later. Although the pain of this double loss was deeply felt by every member of the family, Babcia felt the loss of her older daughter and granddaughter at such a tender age endlessly.

Szczepan - Born December 26, 1905, Died May 16, 1973

Szczepan was deported with us to Siberia. We relied on his acumen and enterprise in our most difficult situations. He served in the Second Polish Corp and saw action in Italy and Normandy. His wife, Marcela, was in the Women's Auxiliary Force and their son, Ignac, in the Cadet Corps. Szczepan always had a positive outlook and was decisive in his actions. After demobilization, he lived in Britain with his family. His son, Ignac, sponsored by Wujek Ludwik, immigrated to Sudbury, Ontario, Canada. Ignac saw the lack of opportunity in Sudbury soon after arriving there and moved to Toronto. There, he married Irena and they had three children – Teresa, Richard and Mark. Ignac was truly a man with a vision and ambition, a clever businessman and extremely hard working. Fortunately, destiny smiled upon him, and due to his hard work and ingenuity, he built a business and factory from nothing. His family still manages this company. His is a wonderful tale of poverty to prosperity because of his intelligence, confidence and charisma.

Adela (Bystryk) – Born December 18, 1907, Died June 4, 1994

My wonderful Mama was a human dynamo, a woman of many talents and keen intuition. Without her quick thinking, resourcefulness and take-charge personality, I don't think our family would have survived the challenges thrown at us. She was decisive, spiritual and always guided by her strong faith in God. However, beneath her strong and resilient character lay a tender heart, always seeking to help others where possible. She was the mother of two children – Henryka (Henia) and Krystyna (Krysia – me).

Aniela (Hanas) – Estimated Year of Birth 1909, Died 1996

Aniela was a housewife, widowed when her husband, Franek, was arrested and killed. She was left to raise her young daughter, Andrzeja (Ania), alone. She stayed in Wroclaw and helped her daughter, Ania, become a professional and pursue her studies as a linguist. Life in Communist Poland was especially difficult for a widow with a child, but our family ties were always very strong. Whenever a family member visited Poland, they would stay in Wroclaw with Aniela or Stenia and their families.

Piotr – Estimated Year of Birth 1911, Estimated Year of Death 1912

We have almost no information about Piotr. We believe that he died of cholera during an epidemic in Eastern Europe.

Bronek – Born May 10, 1914, Died April 20, 1982

He served in the Polish military before the war, which was compulsory. He later became an apprentice to a butcher in Halicz. His goal was to own a deli after completing his training. Deportation interrupted his plans. He served in the Second Corps and drove a jeep down the winding, zigzagging roads in the dark when the Polish forces were storming the Benedictine monastery at Monte Cassino. After demobilization, he worked in a coal mine in Wales. When Bronek expressed the wish to immigrate to Canada to join his younger brother, Ludwik, the necessary documents were completed. Ludwik immediately sponsored his brother. The two brothers shared an apartment in Sudbury. After a few years, Bronek decided to pursue his dream of being a butcher and owning a deli. He and a partner opened the

Deli Market in Sudbury. His business partner did not turn out to be honest. Bronek realized that he was stealing from the profits. They were forced to close their business after a few years. Bronek moved to Toronto and later to Buffalo, New York, after his marriage to Anna. His assistance was invaluable when Mama, Henia, my three-year-old niece, Christine and I relocated to Buffalo from Worcester. He helped us find a two-family house just around the block from his own home and continued to advise us in a variety of ways. He helped us to settle in and made the move to our new environment easier. I am extremely grateful for his patient and thoughtful advice. He was always upbeat and had a positive outlook on life and the future. He was extremely industrious and optimistic and devoted to our family. For example, often, after a long day at his own job, he would pick up Henia from the downtown store where she worked to drive her home so that she did not have to take the bus alone after dark. Bronek had a keen wit, always ready with a joke and a smile. He was very kind and patient with my niece who spent much time at Bronek and Anna's home. He also took seriously his responsibility as the stepfather of Anna's teen-age son from a previous marriage.

Jozef (Jozek) – Born March 23, 1916, Died April 7, 2000

Jozek also served in the Polish military for two years, as was compulsory. He pursued studies in agronomy after his discharge. He secretly slipped away from the freight wagon during the family's forced deportation to Siberia from our home in Ostoja. When he returned to his village, he realized that it would be impossible to stay because of the neighbors' hostility, so he moved to a larger city in Poland and continued his studies. Jozek married a woman named Krysia and had two children – Adam and Barbara (Basia). The possibility of immigrating to Canada arose after Ludwik's encouragement and visit to Poland. Jozek settled in Toronto and became a homeowner. He always enjoyed gardening and carpentry as a hobby. He adjusted well to life as a Canadian citizen. Jozek was also my godfather. Due to concerns over my prospects, he consistently encouraged me to continue my education, which had ended when my father suddenly passed away shortly after I graduated from high school. To please Jozek, I registered at the community college and was pleasantly surprised that my lack of confidence did not equate with a lack of aptitude. Without his confidence in my abilities and best wishes for my future, I may not have enrolled in the community college, which turned out to be the first step in my further education. I am endlessly grateful to him and admire his kind, good-natured attitude toward life's challenges. In later years, Jozek continued his carpentry hobby, building intricate dollhouses for his great-nieces, which remain treasured possessions that they passed on to their own children.

Tadeusz – Estimated Year of Birth 1918, Estimated Death 1920

Tadeusz tragically died at the age of two from an influenza epidemic that devastated many families in Ostoja. Mama, along with other family members, never ceased to grieve and feel the painful loss of their blond, curly-haired, angel brother. His name was always mentioned with deep emotion.

Stefania (Kieruczenko Avramenko) – Born March 23, 1920, Died February 24, 1998

Stenia accompanied Jozek when he left the boxcar on its way to Siberia. They returned to Ostoja. She also realized that they could not remain there because of the hostility of the Ukrainian neighbors, fomented by Soviet propaganda. She ultimately settled in the larger city of Wroclaw with her sister, Aniela, and niece, Ania. They were each other's confidantes and support system. Stenia became an accomplished tailor and dressmaker, so skilled at her craft that she could create beautiful clothing simply by looking at a photograph and fabric. She married Mikolaj, an electrical engineer, and they had a son, Andrzej (Andrew). Sadly, Mikolaj died at a young age from cancer. Life in Communist Poland was difficult, with shortages and the general restraints imposed on citizens. Ludwik, who was her twin brother, came to visit her after she was widowed, and plans were made for her to immigrate to Canada. Yet again, Ludwik stepped up to the plate, sponsoring Stenia and Andrzej. Life in Toronto presented challenges for Stenia and her son, but after acclimating to the new country, Stenia opened a successful dressmaking and alterations store in Toronto. Andrew graduated from the University of Toronto's respected engineering program and later became a senior executive at a well-known aeronautics company. Visiting Stenia was always a pleasure! Even the family's young children were charmed by her and looked forward to the visits that were filled with laughter and good food. She had an engaging, happy, sincere personality, but she was always able to speak directly and get to the heart of the matter.

Ludwik – Born March 23, 1920, Died June 8, 1983

Ludwik, a soldier in the Carpathian Brigade, was in Italy when the fierce fight for Europe's freedom ensued. In 1945, after the signing of the Yalta Treaty that gave away 20 percent of Poland's eastern territories to the Soviet regime, Ludwik could not see himself returning to Poland under the Communist regime. Communist domination was unacceptable to Ludwik. When Canada agreed to welcome four thousand veterans on a two-year work contract obligation, Ludwik decided to pursue this opportunity. He worked for a rancher in Saskatchewan. He worked from sunup to sundown, tending 922 cows and 40 horses, for only forty-five dollars per month. Although he knew that he was seriously overworked, language barriers and the remoteness of the ranch presented significant obstacles. Ludwik courageously contacted the Selective Service Agency, whose responsibilities included the welfare of new immigrants. The rancher lost an excellent worker and hopefully had an epiphany regarding his conscienceless exploitation of a young man in a difficult position. Ludwik was transferred to a second and then a third ranch. The third rancher, N., was an honorable man, and seeing that Ludwik was a trustworthy, hardworking man, agreed to pay him seventy-five dollars per month. After observing how diligently the young man worked, the ranch owner, of his own volition, further increased Ludwik's monthly compensation to one hundred dollars per month. When his work contract expired, Ludwik relocated to Sudbury, Ontario. INCO, a Canadian mining company, offered employment. He married Daniela, and they had two children – Karen and George. Ludwik worked at INCO for thirty-three years. Unfortunately, he was exposed to carcinogenic elements, developed cancer, and died at the age of sixty-three.

Ludwik's commitment to his family made it possible for two of his brothers, one sister, one sister-in-law, three nephews, one niece and others – a total of eleven people – to immigrate to Canada. He personally took care of all the formalities and was the reason they could escape Communism's totalitarian control and improve their lives in a new country. His efforts made it possible for all their children to be successful engineers, doctors and designers.

Babcia's children personified the best in Polish tradition. They learned to persevere when destiny devised difficulties. They attempted to establish stability and reinstitute a normal life without delays or complaints. Our life frequently involved cruel thunderstorms, with dark clouds obstructing the light. Sunshine sometimes broke through, and rainbows offered hope. Babcia's children possessed the ability to accept and allow disappointments to be lessons from which they evolved and grew.

Life's irony, however, separated the siblings for many years. Circumstances, at times, forced them to live divergent lives – some in their Communist-controlled homeland and some in democratic Canada and the United States. We are grateful that their faith sustained and guided them to safer shores. Distance or geography never diminished the abiding love that they shared for each other until the end of their lives. They never ceased to be devoted to each other, always concerned for each other and supportive in whatever manner possible. It's mystifying how destiny tossed them into unforeseen situations, burdening their hearts with a mixture of emotions consisting of distress, concern and hope. Divine Providence, however, separated them physically for eternity: Babcia buried in Africa, with half her children in Poland and half in foreign countries, an ocean away. Fate made the last determination.

A wise, spiritual philosopher claimed the place that we find ourselves at any moment is the place God circled for us on the globe. In other words, nothing is left to chance. This belief makes acknowledgement of their difficult situations easier.

When I reflect on the lives of my relatives, I realize that these were the "salt of the earth" – wonderful human beings. A passage from Scripture that has always made a profound impression on me is 2 Timothy 4:6: "I have fought the good fight, I have finished the race, and I have kept the faith." This passage perfectly articulates the spirit and lives of Babcia's children.

Karolina at her father's funeral.

Stanislaw in uniform in the center with two friends. 8 March 1936.

Adela, my beloved Mama, 15 February 1944.

Szczepan and Marcela in uniform. England 25 October 1945.

Aniela in Poland. 1950s.

Bronek in uniform.

Jozek holding his daughter Basia.
Toronto, February 1960.

Stenia.

Ludwik in uniform. 30 October 1946.

From left: Stenia, Ania, Jozek, Ludwik and Aniela.
Wroclaw, Poland 31 May 1958.

A TRIBUTE TO MAMA

WAR HAD TAKEN and an enormous, traumatic physical and emotional toll on millions of people. It left a deep, black hole in Poland, a country decimated beyond belief, and in families and individuals worldwide. The stories of many of those unfortunate enough to experience any part of this lamentable saga remain untold. Now is the time to document for future generations these authentic incredible experiences before the last of those who remember are also no longer with us. There are lessons to be learned by future generations so that similar tragedies are not repeated.

Our vagabond life presented many dangers, difficulties and challenges. Yet we, Henia and I, the children, felt safe in spite of any unsettling circumstances, because there was someone totally dedicated to our safety and well-being – our amazing, wonderful Mama. We were certain that she would keep us safe from any harm. She lovingly hovered over us, always vigilant and ready to deflect the darts life aimed at her children. Our unsung hero – our dear Mama.

A question comes to mind. How was a young woman (after all, Mama was only thirty-two years old) able to accurately assess various circumstances and make judgments advantageous to her family's safety and well-being? The answer is rudimentary. My mother possessed an innate intelligence and wisdom passed on through DNA that was explicitly inherent in her personality. This is demonstrated by the satchel filled with important documents and pictures that Mama protected and carried during our complicated odyssey over five continents to preserve our family history and legacy. It is my conviction that anyone connected to her and the other exceptional individuals, whose character I have briefly sketched in this memoir, should feel fortunate to share some of their attributes and use them to their advantage.

Reflecting on the lives of my parents and their siblings, we can see that from childhood, their lives were filled with obstacles, difficulties and deprivation. Yet despite this adversity, they chose to live in dignity and faith. It speaks volumes regarding their noble characters and how they truly were part of the "Greatest Generation."

After retiring, Mama continued Babcia's traditions. Each day began not only with prayer but also with Mass. Even the smallest gift was always acknowledged and appreciated. Mama was very industrious, having had chores and responsibilities since early childhood. Babcia was raising her large family without modern conveniences and every family member had to pitch in. Being idle is something Mama could not tolerate. Sewing, working on alterations for dresses, blouses and skirts purchased on clearance, often kept Mama busy. Her pension was small, so smart financial management was needed. She was also civic minded and belonged to several organizations, including the Propagation of Faith, the Library Circle, and the Veterans Organization. She subscribed to several religious periodicals. She personally sewed numerous dance costumes for the Polish folkdance group Mloda Polonia, to which her granddaughter Christine belonged.

Mama was elated when Polish Cardinal Karol Wojtyla became Pope John Paul II. A group of parishioners were traveling to Rome for the Papal Inauguration. Mama could not miss such a unique occasion. Adventurous even in her seventies, Mama felt that God had rewarded Poland for centuries of faithful devotion to Christianity under impossibly difficult Communist occupation. Mama was in St. Peter's Square for this once-in-a-lifetime inspiring celebration and experienced this joyous, positive, exciting energy with thousands of pilgrims.

Each evening after dinner, Mama watched the local and international news. Being informed about world affairs was very important to her.

Over the years, Mama and I made several trips to Poland. The first was in 1963. We visited Ciocia Aniela, Ciocia Stenia and Wujek Jozek, who had remained in Poland during World War II. We saw them when the Communist government finally allowed relatives to visit. It was an emotional reunion for all of us.

Each time as we began our descent and the pilot announced we would be landing at Warsaw International Airport, a powerful emotion rose in our hearts and tears welled in our eyes. Many times, we had doubted that we would ever be able to visit the country of our birth. Hitler had vowed to wipe Poland off the map. Stalin had forcibly ejected us. Poland was, however, beloved and defended by our ancestors. With every visit, we were drawn, as if by a powerful magnet, to the shrine of the Czarna Madonna, the Black Madonna at Czestochowa, to express gratitude that the incredible circumstances of our life had not destroyed us or our faith. We were able to endure it all, because we were under her protection.

Henia and Mama. 1956.

Krysia and Mama. 1961.

Mama, Henia and Christine. Buffalo 1982.

SZCZESNY FAMILY

ON AUGUST 5, 1967, I married Jan Szczesny. Jan was also from Poland, but his journey to the United States was not as twisted and complicated as mine. Jan and his family – including father Josef, mother Antonina and younger brother Leon – lived in Poland when World War II began.

Josef Szczesny was born May 22, 1882, in Polish territory under Russian domination. He was the oldest of seven children in a land-owner's family. Military service in the czar's army was compulsory. Josef was an excellent specimen of a soldier: over six feet tall, well-built, strong, and even-tempered. He was conscripted to the Imperial Russian Navy, where he served for twenty-five years. He sailed the proverbial seven seas, which opened the world to him. He was ex-posed to a myriad of experiences, which gave him the opportunity to learn many skills. His favorite pastime was reading and writing in Russian. When his ship docked near the Polish border, he took advantage of Russian political turmoil and, not feeling any loyalty to the Bolshevik cause, abandoned the navy to return to his village. In 1925, he married Antonina Soroczynski, who was much younger than he. Josef had saved money while in the navy, purchased several acres of land and became a farmer. Political and social dissatisfaction had led to a change in government. Now the Communist ideology, that everyone was equal, was heard everywhere. The slogan sounded much better than actually living under its precepts. There were always those who were more privileged and wealthier.

Josef's village became part of the collective farm system. A com-mittee was elected, decisions were made, and quotas were set. Each farmer was required to contribute a percentage of their harvest to the Communist Regime as a tax. When the harvest was good, this was not a problem, and there was enough food left for the family. It was a different situation in bad times, when a drought or unexpected occurrence meant there wasn't enough to honor the quota and nothing was left for the family. No excuses were accepted, and punishment was imposed for noncompliance. What a system. Human rights were not respected.

Josef and Antonina's family was blessed with the birth of two sons, Jan in 1929 and Leonard in 1931. The Communist regime made their lives more difficult with each passing month. Each village had a committee, and their responsibility was to elect the manager of the *kolhoz*, collective farm. That person would be responsible for the successes and failures of the *kolhoz*. In April 1933, Josef was unanimously elected the new manager because he could read and write Russian. He had to accept this assignment. Refusal meant disloyalty and being labeled as an enemy of the state and was punishable by imprisonment. This "honor" of becoming the manager proved disastrous for Josef. Less than two months later, in June 1933, he was found negligent because the orchard did not produce a good harvest. Rabbits had damaged the bark on trees, impacting the harvest and the quota to the State could not be met. They needed a "fall guy," and Josef was chosen. There was a trial, and the verdict was calamitous to the family. Josef was pronounced guilty of negligence, punishable by five years of hard labor in a camp for criminals in the Kamchatka Peninsula. He had committed no crime. Is poor harvest truly a crime? Innocent people filled Soviet prisons under this flawed ideology. No consideration was given to how the family would survive without its main breadwinner. The entire family was being punished. Josef traveled for two months by train to reach the Kamchatka Peninsula Labor Camp, thousands of miles from home. He worked twelve-hour shifts cutting down trees and sending logs down the river. He was a model worker, and because of his cooperation and industry, he was released four months sooner than the specified sentence. During his absence, Antonina had to fulfill the work requirements for the four people in the family. Their grandmother, Michalina, lived with them and helped to take care of Jan and Leon, who were only four and three years old when their father was imprisoned. All had to deflect disparaging remarks from neighbors and classmates. Only with God's grace was the family able to survive this unjust penalty. When Josef was released from prison, the family traveled many days by train through Russia to rejoin him. Because Josef was not allowed to come within one hundred kilometers of his village, he had to find employment and reestablish the family in Russia. This was difficult because he was labeled a criminal. The turmoil created by the war made it possible for the Szczesny family to return to Poland. For a while, they lived in Poland as farmers until they were rounded up by the German army during World War II.

The Germans utilized a practice of rounding up families off the street and transporting them to Germany to work in munition factories as slave laborers. This allowed German men to serve in the army. The Gestapo brought the people who were designated to fulfill the forced labor quota to the railway station to be loaded into freight wagons. In their case, the Szczesny family was sent to Iserlohn, in the province of Westphalia. The trip to their destination lasted eight days. The freight wagons were locked from the outside with the future slave laborers inside.

When they arrived at Iserlohn, they were assigned one room in a wooden housing barrack belonging to the munition factory. The boys, only thirteen and twelve years old, were forced to work twelve-hour shifts in the factory. Since Jan was a minor, the Germans did not document his employment, and he later was never compensated for his work. Iserlohn was their residence from 1943 until May 2, 1945. They were liberated by the American army after Germany surrendered and the war ended. After liberation, they moved to a refugee camp, and eventually the boys, Jan and Leon, attended school. Returning to Poland under the Communist regime was totally unacceptable. Their plan, therefore, was to immigrate to the United States, sponsored by the Catholic Relief Organization where they hoped to attain a stable life that offered opportunities. U.S. government requirements had to be met before anyone could immigrate, including passing a physical exam and various health and mental assessments and having no criminal record and a sponsor to help the new arrivals settle in. When all their prerequisites were completed, Jan was ready for his voyage to the New World. He disembarked in New York City, where a representative from Ford Motor Company was scouting new employees. Jan and a few others passengers on the ship were immediately offered a job. Jan signed the contract, and two days later he was at the Ford Stamping Plant in Lackawanna, New York. The twenty-two-year-old immigrant faced the sobering realization that he was now alone in Buffalo. He had no family to count on for help, little knowledge of the English language, and only a few dollars in his wallet, but a dream in his heart gave him courage. He had to rely on his own ingenuity and industry to achieve his goals and to reunite the family in Buffalo. Forging ahead with a positive attitude, Jan worked extra hours and days to earn as much money as possible. The work was physical, as there was no automation or robots; these came later. The young man was a sports enthusiast. Soccer games and practice took time from work but offered diversion and a chance to socialize after games. Jan became a member of the White Eagles Soccer League. Many games were held in different cities. The teams were ethnic based – Italian, German, Hungarian, Macedonian, et cetera. Competition was fierce, and ethnic pride was involved. In the summer, Sunday afternoons were spent at league matches. The spectators were instigators, and there were often calls of "kick the so-and-so" and "break his leg," which resulted in serious confrontations. One Sunday in July, the White Eagles were playing a match with a rival German team in Jamestown. Jan was an excellent player with quick reflexes and accurate aim that hurled the soccer ball where he planned. The German team was losing, and the players were angry. Jan kicked the ball and slipped. A player from the opposing team intentionally and maliciously jumped on Jan's outstretched leg and broke his shin in several places.

The ambulance took Jan to the hospital, where he remained for several days. Swelling prevented an accurate diagnosis of the injury and delayed applying the cast. This was an extremely difficult situation for someone without the support of family to offer help and emotional encouragement. The bone was not mending properly, and a later infection complicated the healing process. Further surgery became necessary. Metal pins had to be inserted to hold the broken bones in place until they bonded. The convalescent period stretched into many months. Before the accident, Jan could be counted on to provide rides to games, picnics, and beaches for his friends. Now he needed help, and this proved to be a test of who were his real friends. Many didn't take the opportunity to visit and cheer up their dejected teammate in need of company. The process of earning extra money and accelerating the realization of his plan slowed drastically.

Nine years later, after becoming a citizen, Jan was able to bring his parents and brother to live in the United States. He purchased a house. But when he counted the money for a down payment, he was dismayed to realize that he was $1,200 short. So, close, but still not enough. Fortunately, a good friend, Stasis, loaned him the amount needed, and a brand-new, three-bedroom brick ranch became the family's dream residence. Antonina was overjoyed, envisioning a comfortable, stable life on the horizon. She was full of hope, with plans to furnish their home and to buy curtains. Sadly, her dream was not realized. Six months later, the completely heartbroken family was making Antonina's funeral arrangements. She passed away at only fifty-five years of age. Life had thrown them another curve. This pain would take years to subside and accept.

Another unwelcome complication was that Josef's X-ray showed a spot on his lung. The health officials were afraid that it could be tuberculosis. Josef was required to undergo a series of intense health tests and compulsory stay in a hospital in Perry, New York, for one year. This was for observation and to detect any changes in future X-rays. The spot on Josef's lung was a calcification from a lung infection (most likely pneumonia), which had happened decades before. The doctors were overly cautious, but the requirement had to be obeyed.

The hoped-for American dream was at times elusive and full of thorns: the father in a hospital sixty miles away from Buffalo, waiting for his sons to visit; the son, working extra hours to pay for the mortgage and funeral debt. When Josef was discharged from the hospital and came home, he assumed the duties of cooking, cleaning, doing the laundry and gardening. Before his discharge, Leon had been the chef. Slowly, life and their future became more hopeful.

In 1967, after Jan and I married, we lived in the very house that Jan purchased for his family. In 1963, Leon married Anne Strzelczyk, and they moved into a new house that shared its backyard with the family home. Josef lived with Jan and our family until he died in 1982. Josef missed the centenarian birthday celebration that the family had planned for him by a little more than two weeks in May 1982. He received a congratulatory letter from then President Ronald Regan, which still hangs framed on the wall, although the festivities were not held. The Szczesny's had become adept at transcending the difficulties in their lives.

This brief narrative of the Szczesny family showed how they were severely tested, endured with God's help, and could lead comfortable lives in the United States. Horrendous life experiences did not leave them bitter or angry, just grateful and appreciative for the opportunities that came later.

Krysia teaching at Buffalo Public School 57, Grades 2 and 3, 1976-77.

Szczesny Family, from left, Antonina, Jan, Josef and Leon in Germany, late 1940s.

Krysia and Jan's wedding, August 5, 1967 on the steps of
St. Stanislaus Church in Buffalo, NY

Krysia & Jan's Wedding. From left: Basia, Anna, Daniela, Bronek, Ludwik,
Mama, Andrew, me (Krysia), Jan, Adam, Henia, Jozek, Stenia and Krysia.
Christine, 6 years old, standing in front.

Three generations – Josef, Jan and Greg. 1970.

Three generations – Jan, Greg & son Justin. 2002.

BUFFALO

JAN AND I bought a house and settled in Cheektowaga, New York. We were blessed with a son, Greg, and a daughter, Ursula (nicknamed Ula).

In 1994, Jan retired from the Ford Stamping Plant after forty years of service. I retired in 1995, completing twenty-nine years of service in the Buffalo Public School System. I was in the trenches working with disadvantaged youth, striving to make an impact on their academic development.

The retirement that we enjoyed was the result of the lessons learned in the so-called University of Hard Knocks, through adversity to a stable, peaceful and comfortable everyday life. We were always budget conscious and planned well. This allowed us to enrich our retirement by traveling to many exciting countries and exotic places. We traveled to every continent and almost every country in Europe with friends or with our children. We visited France, including Lourdes; Italy, including Rome and the Vatican; Poland and Czestochowa many times; Portugal, including Fatima; Greece, including Athens, the Parthenon, and many islands; and several places in Russia. We even traveled to Yalta, where the Yalta Treaty was signed. In the Middle East, we visited Israel, seeing the Wailing Wall, Nazareth, and Bethlehem; Greg and Ula waded in the Jordan River; we visited Jordan, including Petra and the Wadi Desert; and Turkey. In Africa, we visited Egypt and went inside the pyramids, traveled by camel, and sailed the Nile. We traveled to Morocco, Algiers, Ghana, Liberia, Nigeria, Gabon, Namibia, South Africa, Kenya, and Djibouti and sailed through the Suez Canal. We traveled to Australia, New Zealand, Bora Bora, Fiji, American Samoa, and places that most people only read about in National Geographic. In the Orient, we were in Hong Kong, walked the Great Wall of China, visited Tiananmen Square, and in Japan, we visited Nagasaki and Hiroshima. We also traveled to India, South Korea, Vietnam, Thailand, Malaysia, Singapore and the Philippines. We traveled to many countries in Central and South America, including Costa Rica, Nicaragua, Guatemala, Venezuela, Peru, including Machu Picchu, and Chile. Some of these were leisurely cruises, other guided bus tours. We also traveled extensively throughout the United States, including Alaska, where we saw glaciers and Denali.

We traveled with many of our friends who were also immigrants and shared similar experiences and interests. One of these friends was T., a survivor of the Dachau concentration camp. He was only fifteen and tattooed with a camp number. This was strange for a Catholic but war was cruel to many, not just Jews. As many as 3 million Polish Catholics were interned in concentration camps. His wife had experiences similar to mine. She had also been deported to Siberia and spent six years in East Africa. Most of the couples we traveled with had been in German labor camps. We have been friends for over fifty years now, sharing joyous and sad experiences. Our friends have been as precious as gold. Empathy proved to be our strong "golden bond."

Now our children are adults. We are extremely proud of our children. They are part of the future of our nation. Their achievements fill our hearts with pride. Henia's daughter, Christine, is a highly respected attorney, holding a senior position in the federal government. Greg is an independent long-distance truck owner and operator. Ula earned both structural and mechanical engineering degrees. Few women enter that arena, let alone earn two degrees. Additionally, she holds an advanced degree in pedagogy and six math and science teaching certifications, performing work that will benefit future generations while raising her lovely family.

The DNA passed on by our amazing ancestors gave them the aptitude and the drive to persevere, as well as the determination to advance and expand their possibilities to create fulfilling careers. Some say that if you dream big, you can achieve what seems impossible. I wholeheartedly agree, and I think my family would too.

Our grandchildren are extremely perceptive and diligent. Although young, they already personify the qualities and values of Babcia's children. They show interest in pursuing professions that will benefit society and give them personal satisfaction. They are fortunate to have parents with high principles who will guide them through life's obstacles. My hope for my grandchildren is that they learn from their ancestors to work hard and never give up on achieving their dreams.

I am certain that whoever had contact with us, at work and in our daily lives, would be extremely surprised to learn how close we came to losing our lives because of starvation, deprivation and perilous situations. Our positive attitude and joy belied our previous circumstances. We assimilated well into the community and are grateful for the opportunities available to us in our new, stable country. We had ambition and worked hard to acquire and excel at our professions.

The driving force now, as then, is our faith, gratitude and appreciation for small or big chances. Instinctively, we lived by the axiom that seasoned sailors follow to survive – "no one can control the wind, but we can and need to adjust our sails to endure in dangerous situations." That is what we did. As we sailed through dangerous, angry storms, we kept adjusting our sails so that we wouldn't perish in the thunderstorms of our lives. We were determined not to allow the angry gales to push us off course and to keep us from reaching our goals.

Now, arriving at our "golden years," we thought that we had overcome all our difficulties. But this wasn't the case. For almost three years, Jan has been a resident at a memory care facility. His memory loss, combined with being unable to walk after breaking his hip and other medical conditions, forced this decision. We had to accept this significant convolution in our retirement and cope to the best of our abilities. Complaining is a waste of energy, and soliciting God's help and guidance provides us an optimistic outlook. Once again, the power of our faith calms our fears, gives us hope and sustains us.

A quote from Albert Einstein that resonates with me is "You can believe that there are no miracles or that everything good in your life is a miracle." I live by this mantra. I believe many of the incredible milestones of my and my family's lives were nothing short of miracles.

We were hoping that the golden years of our retirement were here for good. Unanticipated circumstances tested our resilience. Emotion-filled decisions were required for a beneficial resolution for all concerned. Our faith continues to sustain us and has quieted our fears. Providence gives us fortitude and steers us on an ethical path. All this will pass. We already see rainbows on the horizon.

Henia with daughter Christine and granddaughter Rachael, 1986.

Henia, Jonathan (Christine's husband), Christine and daughter Rachael
at Jan's 80th Birthday party, 2009.

Family picture, Greg and Sherry with their kids, Chelsea and Justin,
March 27, 2005.

Family picture, Ursula and Craig with their kids,
Jacob (standing behind Ursula), Marek and Julia

Family picture at St. John Kanty Church, May 19, 2007.

Family picture at my house, Christmas 2007.

Krysia on one of her three trips to Egypt with friends and family.

Krysia and Jan cruising the South Pacific with friends, Feb 1994.

**Krysia and friends at the Peace Park statue in Nagasaki Japan.
Part of their Far East cruise, 1995.**

Krysia, fourth from the left. Janek, second from the left, with friends in Petra Jordan while on a Mediterranean cruise, 1996.

Krysia, in cowboy hat, with friends walking the Great Wall of China.
An excursion on their cruise from China to India.

On our couch with the grandkids, from left, Jacob, Julia, Marek,
Chelsea and Justin. 2008.

WHY THIS BOOK CAME ABOUT

I WAS ORIGINALLY motivated to share our family's incredible voyage because I found a hand-written memoir written by Mama when she was eighty-two years old. It is impressive that she could remember events in proper sequence, naming dates and places as they were indelibly etched in her memory. In fact, she spent countless nights writing her memoir at the kitchen table. I feel that I am meant to complete her monumental undertaking. In writing this memoir, I seek to honor her efforts and express deep pride and appreciation to my family, my companions on this perilous journey – especially to my Mama and Tata, my Babcia, and my many *Wujeks* for the vigilant and loving care that made it possible for me, a three-year-old, my sister, Henia, and a cousin, Ignac, to survive the horrendous circumstances that made the narrative of this inordinate human tragedy possible.

I am certain that my mother had an ulterior motive for expending so much time and energy on the chronicle of this calamity. She was extremely proud of her hero brothers and husband, the veterans. After all, it was their valiant military service that secured the peace in the world that we enjoyed for many years. I believe that it was her wish that younger generations be inspired by her husband, her brothers, and her sisters to strive to live their lives by the same high standards.

Some of the younger members of my family are unaware of the scope of twists and turns in the lives of their parents, grandparents and great-grandparents or the path that brought them to the United States and Canada. The adults who experienced the extraordinary tragedies didn't talk much about this complicated road and didn't question the Providence that put them there. The motivation behind this silence can be analyzed by psychiatrists at a later time. Ferocious winds of

191

war buffeted these noble individuals from the beginning of their lives. Yet when God calmed the storm and the sun shone to illuminate the road forward, the future appeared smooth and positive. Poverty and tragedy taught us to be happy with very little. Experiences related to war or other dramatic events in our lives created a state of mind seldom found in people living under normal conditions. When our terrible conditions improved, we were grateful and didn't feel bitter or disillusioned.

Unfortunately, I am now the only surviving member of our family who experienced this calamity. I feel a sense of obligation to memorialize the places, dates, and specifics of our journey so that they are not forgotten. The nightmare of banishment from our home, deportation to the wilderness of Siberia, through the steppes of Kazakhstan and the seemingly endless treks by the train were traumatic. We believed fervently that God's gift of mercy would prevail through all our difficulties and would point the way out of the maze.

With my mother's journal and Henia's recollection, I began to write this memoir. Tomorrow is not promised to anyone, and I am the only survivor, so there is no time to waste. Although I was a novice, I proceeded to write with Ula's help. Several months after I started this memoir, Henia's health unexpectedly deteriorated rapidly. After a stay in the hospital, surrounded by those most dear to her, Henia was called by our Creator to her Eternal Reward. She was our champion and irreplaceable – compassionate, dependable, devoted to the family, quick with a smile and good advice – and she was a dear sister, beloved mother to Christine, grandmother to Rachael, aunt to Greg and Ula, and great-aunt to Chelsea, Justin, Jacob, Marek and Julia. This monumental loss crushed our spirits and filled our hearts and our lives with pain and sadness, delaying the completion of this memoir. She was my one and only sister. My dedicated guardian and protector from my youth, she made a final exit much too suddenly. Henia and I were always there for each other. We never had a serious argument, just an occasional difference of opinion, which we accepted as a different point of view on situations. Our unconditional love over many decades remains an unbreakable bond.

When I was younger and an inquisitive child, Henia, ten years older, was vigilant for my safety and on occasion would remark, "I always wished to have a sister, and you are so much trouble!" "Don't go there!" "Come home now!" "What compelled you to do that?" "You always get into my things and leave a mess." These sentiments were fleeting and quickly forgotten, replaced by our love and concern for each member of our family.

Our journey took us through several countries, continents, time zones, and climates. We used many modes of transportation – sleigh, oxen-pulled wagon, boxcar, freight wagon, freighter, vessel, trucks, buses, passenger trains, barges and ships – and none were comfortable. Cold, hungry, and dirty for days, we didn't have the facilities for a bath or change of clothes. Nevertheless, we always felt that the Almighty Hand, the Good Shepard from the Scripture, guided our steps and kept us from falling into despair. We had a vision for a happier tomorrow and were encouraged when favorable possibilities for a better future appeared. We are grateful to our adopted countries for giving us a chance to finally live in a stable environment. We are enjoying the privileges that U.S. and Canadian citizens enjoy. We did it all on our own. We never received any assistance from anyone, just an opportunity.

Many labels were used to describe us – deportees, slave laborers, exiles, refugees, displaced persons, immigrants. We happily answer to one:

SURVIVORS.

A longstanding family tradition has been to wish a departing person *"Idz z Bogiem,"* meaning "Go with God" or "God speed." I have said this innumerable times to my sister, children, relatives and friends. It is my wish and prayer for the reader of this memoir to continue your journey guided and protected by God. I bid you "Idz z Bogiem" – may your life be full of joy and the road ahead smooth and carefree.